SOFT FONTS

SOFT FONTS

20 SEWING PROJECTS
with words & letters

Nicola Tedman & Sarah Skeate

GIBBS SMITH
TO ENRICH AND INSPIRE HUMANKIND

First Edition
18 17 16 15 14   5 4 3 2 1

Published by
Gibbs Smith
P.O. Box 667
Layton, Utah 84041

1.800.835.4993 orders
www.gibbs-smith.com

This book was conceived, designed, and produced by

Ivy Press
210 High Street
Lewes
East Sussex BN7 2NS
United Kingdom
www.ivypress.co.uk

Creative Director Peter Bridgewater
Publisher Susan Kelly
Conceived by Sophie Collins
Editorial Director Tom Kitch
Senior Designer James Lawrence
Designer Clare Barber
Photographer Neal Grundy
Illustrator Vicky Woodgate
Models Anna and William Stevens

Ivy Press would like to thank Dan Gneiding for permission to use his font Ribbon and Peter Fritzsche for permission to use his font Origami.

Printed and bound in China

ISBN: 978-1-4236-3492-8

Library of Congress Control Number: 2013948626

Contents

Before You Start

The projects in this book include accessories you can make from scratch, as well as inspirational ideas for personalizing existing items. The designs vary in complexity so even if you're relatively inexperienced there will be plenty for you to make, but read this section before you start on your first project—you'll find it useful in helping you get the best possible finish.

FINDING FONTS

The fonts we've suggested you use are a mixture of those that may have come bundled with your computer's operating system and others that can be purchased online.

A few projects use specific words or phrases, and templates have been supplied for these. In other cases, you're free to choose your own initials or letters. Once you've established the font you want to use and loaded it on your computer, type the characters in the correct font in your word processing or desktop publishing program, then simply change the font size to fit the project. Most programs offer onscreen rulers or the option of viewing your work in a print layout view so you can scale your font's size accurately before printing it out. Instructions are provided for making templates or stencils to use in your chosen project.

EQUIPMENT

You'll only need basic crafting tools and sewing supplies for the majority of these projects, and all have full equipment as well as materials lists at the beginning, so that you can check that you have everything you'll need before you start. Some projects call for you to sew leather or denim, in which case a leather needle for your sewing machine will be necessary.

There are two other pieces of equipment that are called for in a few projects and that may be worth investing in: a laminator and a bias tape maker.

Laminator

A laminator is used to coat a piece of paper or cardboard with flexible plastic. In these projects, its use is sometimes suggested to help you to create hardy templates or stencils that can be used with paint. Laminators and the glue pouches that are used with them are invaluable to enthusiastic crafters, are relatively inexpensive, and are easy to get hold of. If you decide you'd like one, check out the different models and sizes online to get the best deal; you'll find that there are plenty of options. It's worth investing in one of the bigger sizes, because this gives you the option of creating larger templates or stencils.

Bias tape maker

Bias tape makers are small and inexpensive, and can be found online or in the sewing departments in stores. You can buy them to create different widths of tape, but regular sewers may want to own several in different sizes—you simply pull your length of bias-cut fabric through a tape maker and it turns in the edges to create instant bias tape that you can then use for binding edges, making loops, and so on. In this book, you'll find bias tape is also sometimes used to re-create flowing, calligraphic fonts.

TECHNIQUES
Sewing

The projects use both hand and machine sewing. Any special needles—for sewing leather or denim—are mentioned in the materials lists for the projects, which use a wide range of textiles and fabrics.

Hand sewing is generally straightforward. However, you may be unfamiliar with a slip stitch, which is used in a few of the projects. The slip stitch is used to close gaps between two edges of fabric.

To sew the slip stitch, align the two fabric edges and bring the needle up from the wrong side of one piece of fabric, then stitch between the fabrics as shown in the diagram. Sew loosely, pulling the thread up to tighten it every few stitches.

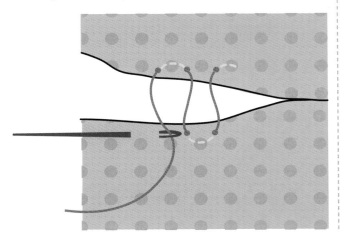

If you are using fusible web, simply hold the iron on the paper for a few seconds, then place it on another part—don't slide the iron around.

Gluing
FUSIBLE WEB

This is used to glue two fabrics together; the type used in this book has an adhesive with paper backing on one side, and it is simply pressed directly onto the wrong side of the fabric you are using (the heat dissolves and activates the glue, so it fuses to the fabric).

FUSIBLE INTERFACING

This is used to stiffen fabrics. The type used in this book has an iron-on adhesive on one side to allow it to be easily applied to fabrics.

GLUE

Two kinds of glue are specified in the projects. One is high-tack craft glue, which is particulary sticky. It's best to use it sparingly and to aim it accurately—a little goes a long way.

The second is contact glue, which has a strong hold provided it's used correctly. Spread a thin layer of glue on both of the surfaces to be glued together (a spatula spreader is useful here; some contact glue comes with one, ready to use), let dry for a minute or two, then press the surfaces firmly together.

{Single-Letter} Tote Bag

There are so many appealing fonts easily available that it can be hard to pick the best for your project. For this simple lettered bag, the letter that you choose must have a shadowed effect, so that you can use two contrasting colors of fabric. If you've only got an hour to spare, this project is a good choice—it's extremely easy and fast to do.

PERSONALIZING YOUR PROJECT

- Once you've mastered a single shadowed letter, try this simple technique for pairs of initials.
- You can also create inline letters by using thin cord sewn within the overall outline.

CHOOSING YOUR LETTER

Although any shadowed font will work for this project, try something simple if it's your first attempt. Below are some possible options.

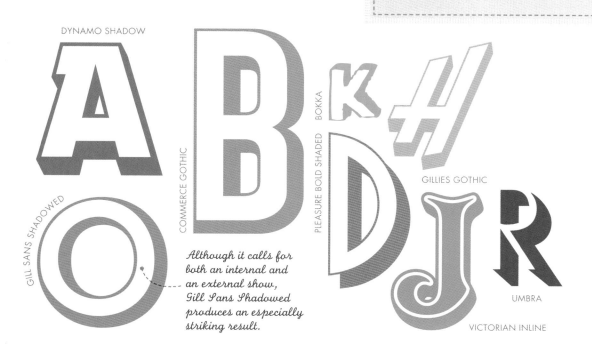

Although it calls for both an internal and an external show, Gill Sans Shadowed produces an especially striking result.

DYNAMO SHADOW

BOKKA

PLEASURE BOLD SHADED

COMMERCE GOTHIC

GILL SANS SHADOWED

GILLIES GOTHIC

UMBRA

VICTORIAN INLINE

Making the tote bag

1 Choose a font for the single letter that you want to use. For this project, you need a shadowed font, so pick one like the examples shown on page 9.

2 To make a template, print out the letter on plain paper, sized to fit one side of the tote bag. For most bags, you'll find that this means that the letter should be around 10 inches (25.5 cm) high.

3 Iron the tote bag. Cut the letter out of the paper and place it on the tote bag, positioning it in the center (use the ruler if you find it hard to do this by eye). When it's placed correctly, make some small marks around the edge of the letter with the fabric marking pen so that you'll be able to position the final letter.

4 Cut up the letter so that you have separate pieces for the body and the shadow. This example has a single piece for the letter and three separate pieces for the shadow. Pin the letter pattern piece to one piece of fabric and the shadow pattern piece or pieces to the other. Draw around them with the fabric marking pen.

2.

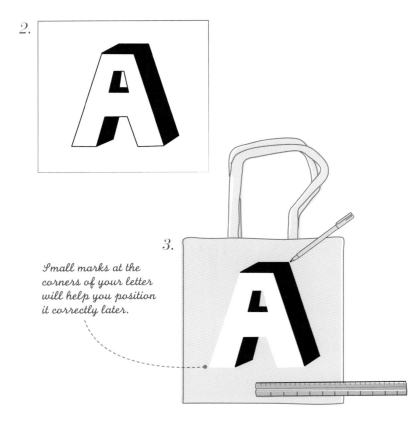

3.

Small marks at the corners of your letter will help you position it correctly later.

4.

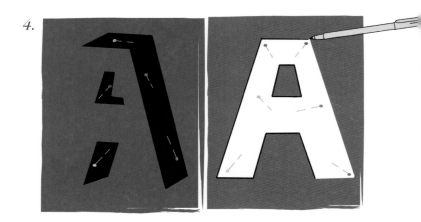

5 Cut the fusible web into two pieces, one for each piece of fabric. Apply the fusible web to the back of each piece of fabric. Cut the letter and shadow pieces out of the fabric.

6 Lay a clean, folded dish towel flat inside your tote bag, and place the bag on the ironing board, with the marked side facing upward. Carefully peel the paper backing off the letter shape and lay it in place on the bag, then press with an iron until it is stuck to the bag. Repeat with the shadow pieces, being careful to align the shadow exactly with the letter.

7 For an especially hard-wearing finish, machine stitch around the edges of the letter, matching the thread to the fabric colors and using a small zigzag stitch.

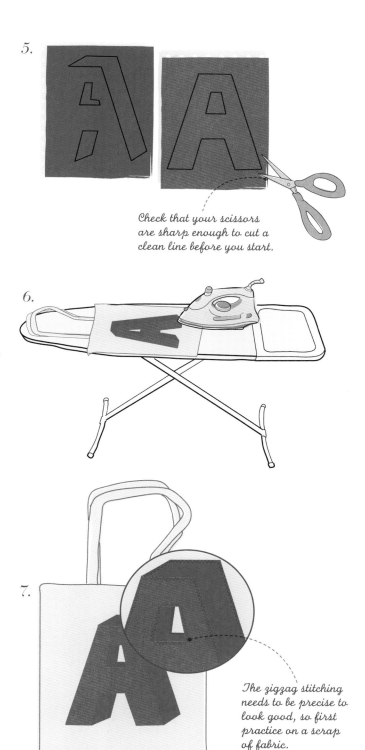

5.

Check that your scissors are sharp enough to cut a clean line before you start.

6.

7.

The zigzag stitching needs to be precise to look good, so first practice on a scrap of fabric.

{Baby} Blocks

Filled with blocks of soft foam and ornamented with a classic font (so they offer a first lesson in good design as well as letter recognition), these alphabet cubes are five times as pretty as anything you'll find in a store. Although they take a little work to arrive at a crisp finished result, you can easily set up a production line to make a full alphabet; a dozen or more blocks are as simple to make as just one or two. Look out for fat-quarter bundles of suitable novelty prints, available from quilting stores and online.

PERSONALIZING YOUR PROJECT

- Instead of using one font with frames, try using a variety of different fonts without frames.
- Replace the novelty fabrics with simple felt outlines of objects stitched onto plain fabrics.

ABOUT THE FONT

bauhaus

Although it was inspired by the work of the Bauhaus designers in the mid-1920s to create an accessible, all-purpose font, the Bauhaus face was actually created in the mid-1970s by the American typographers Ed Benguiat and Victor Caruso.

The clean outlines of the Bauhaus font make the letters easy to cut from felt.

FOR EACH BLOCK YOU WILL NEED

Decorative frame on page 120

½ sheet letter-format inkjet T-shirt transfer paper for light fabrics

Two 5¼-in. (13.5-cm) squares of plain cotton

Two 2¾-in. (7-cm) squares of felt in contrasting colors

Two 5¼-in. (13.5-cm) squares of two different small-print cotton fabrics

Two 5¼-in. (13.5-cm) squares of natural textured linen or cotton

4-in. (10-cm) square of thin cardboard to use as a template

Piece of upholstery foam, 4 in. (10 cm) thick

Stranded embroidery thread to match the felt colors

Sewing thread in a natural color

Embroidery needle

High-tack craft glue

Craft knife

Sharp scissors

Pencil

Fabric marking pen

Metal ruler

Straight pins

Making the blocks

1 Photocopy or scan the decorative frame for the blocks on page 120. Print the frame onto the T-shirt transfer paper, making as many copies as you need (you'll need two frames for each block), then cut out the frames.

2 Following the manufacturer's instructions, iron the T-shirt transfer paper onto the center of each plain cotton square, leaving a ¾-inch (2-cm) gap around the edge of each frame for the border and the seam allowance.

3 Print out your chosen letters onto plain paper with the "b" and "d" 2¼ inches (5.5 cm) high. Cut them out neatly.

4 Pin each letter onto a piece of felt, draw around it using a fabric marking pen, and cut the characters out.

5 Position each felt letter carefully in the center of one of the printed frames and adhere it in place using high-tack craft glue. Leave to dry.

6 Thread an embroidery needle with a single strand of thread to match the felt and hand stitch around the edge of each felt letter, using a small, neat overcast stitch.

1.

2.

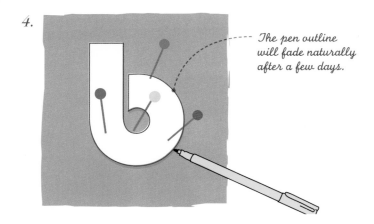

4.

The pen outline will fade naturally after a few days.

7 In addition to the two squares with the frames and letters, for each block you will need one square each of the two small-print patterned fabrics and two squares of the natural textured plain linen or cotton. For each of the six pieces of fabric, place the 4-inch (10-cm) square cardboard template on the center of the wrong side and draw around it with a pencil, adding a ⅝-inch (1.5-cm) seam allowance to each square.

8 Lay out the fabrics in the T-shape shown. Turn them right side down and pin together the centered strip of four squares. If either of your patterned fabrics is directional, you will get the best result if you place the pattern the same way up as the letters.

9 Start to sew your cube together, using ⅝-inch (1.5-cm) seam allowances throughout. Thread your sewing machine with thread in a natural color. Alternating print and letter squares, and starting with a print square, sew the two letter squares and the two print squares into a vertical strip, without stitching into the seam allowance. Make some additional stitches back and forth at the beginning and end of each seam to secure.

10 Stitch one natural linen or cotton square to each side of the top print square on the strip to form a T shape.

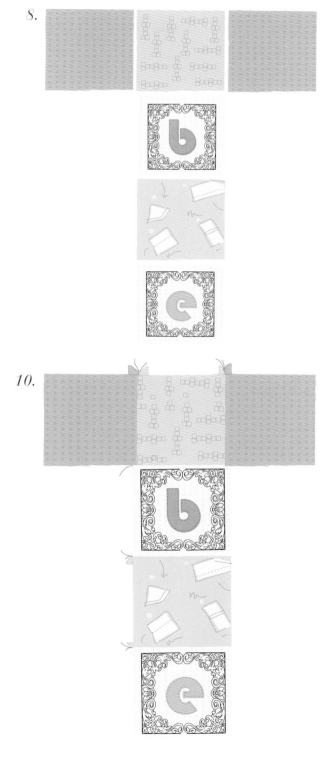

11 Working on the wrong side of the fabrics and pinning before you sew, stitch the next side of each of the linen squares to the sides of the closest letter square.

12 Repeat, sewing the next side of each of the linen squares to the second print square. When you've sewn all the seams, you will have an open fabric "box" with a lid.

13 Stitch two of the three open sides of the fabric "lid" down, so there is just one edge of the fabric cube open. Trim all the stitched seam allowances by half, then turn the cube right side out.

14 Cut a neat cube of upholstery foam into a 4-inch (10-cm) square, using a craft knife and metal ruler. Compressing it firmly with your fingers, push it into the fabric box, easing the box over the cube to fit it smoothly and get all the corners in place.

15 When the foam is neatly within the fabric, fold in the seam allowance of the open edge and pin it together. Thread the embroidery needle with sewing thread in a natural color and neatly ladder stitch the seam closed.

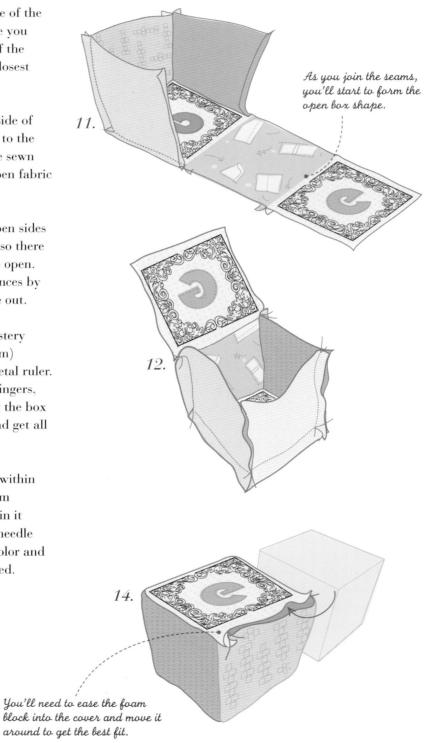

11.

As you join the seams, you'll start to form the open box shape.

12.

14.

You'll need to ease the foam block into the cover and move it around to get the best fit.

Thick, soft felt offers a degree of protection to your tablet computer—and, appliquéd with your initials, identifies it instantly as your property. It's worth tracking down this substantial felt weight, even if it isn't stocked in your local craft outlet; you can find it in various colors online. A dark or neutral color sets off more vibrant initials in a lighter weight of felt—and a wrap-around, legal-style closure to match the initials adds the finishing touch. It's personal, protective, and simple and economical to make.

PERSONALIZING YOUR PROJECT

- Century is a good choice for projects that call for single letters or pairs of initials, but the relatively bulky characters aren't so good for whole words.

ABOUT THE FONT
Century Regular

The original Century type was designed at the end of the nineteenth century by L.B. Benton, and was named for the periodical for which it was commissioned, *Century Magazine*. The commission specifically asked for a bold, legible font, with clean serifs and broad uprights and curves.

The large serifs demand you leave ample space between your letters if you use more than one.

YOU WILL NEED

Template on page 125

24 x 10 in. (61 x 25.5 cm) felt, ³⁄₁₆ in. (5 mm) thick

8-in. (20-cm) square of craft felt in a contrasting color

Sheet of thin cardboard (make sure it's suitable for using with your printer)

8-in. (20-cm) square of fusible web

20-in. (51-cm) length of waxed cotton cord, ¹⁄₁₆ in. (2 mm) in diameter

Two plastic buttons, ¾ in. (2 cm) in diameter, in color to match the craft felt

Topstitch thread to match the thick felt

Sewing thread to match the craft felt

Metal ruler

Craft knife

Sharp scissors

Cutting mat

Pencil

Fabric marking pen or tailor's chalk

Cloth tape measure

Straight pins

Making the case

1 Use the tape measure to measure all around the tablet you're making the case for. Take the exact measurements of both the length and the width.

2 Halve the width measurement and add ½ inch (12 mm) for the seam allowances. Using the craft knife and metal ruler on a cutting mat, cut the thick felt strip to this width.

3 Use the tape measure to transfer the complete length measurement—around both the front and back of the long side of the tablet as well as the ends—to the felt strip, and mark the top end with pins.

4 Photocopy or scan the template on page 125, enlarging it to match the width of your felt strip, then print and cut it out. Pin it to the felt, immediately above the line of pins that you used to mark the top of the case.

5 Cut around the curve of the flap neatly with sharp scissors.

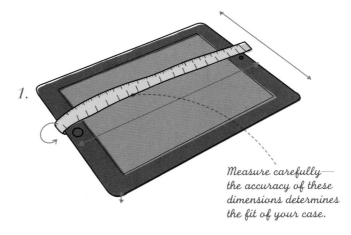

1.

Measure carefully—the accuracy of these dimensions determines the fit of your case.

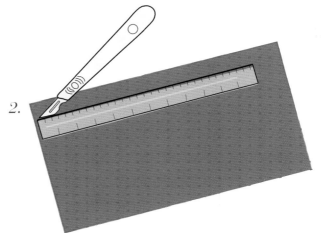

2.

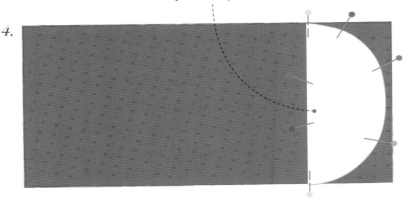

Align the straight edge of the flap exactly with the pin markers.

4.

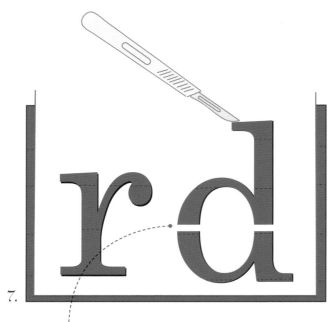

6 Bring the lower edge of the strip up to meet the pins at the bottom of the flap. Press the fold at the bottom of the cover firmly with your fingers and mark it with pins, then unfold the strip.

7 Print out onto thin cardboard the letters you have chosen at a size where they are 1½ inches (4 cm) narrower than the width of the felt strip. Using a craft knife on a cutting mat, cut the letters out, leaving small strips to hold the centers of the letters in place, if necessary.

8 Following the manufacturer's instructions, apply fusible web to the wrong side of the craft felt.

9 Reverse the cardboard stencil, draw your letters on the paper backing of the fusible web with a pencil, and cut them out.

10 Peel the backing paper off the fusible web. Using the stencil to check that they're level and the right distance apart, position the letters on the front of the case, ¾ inch (2 cm) above the fold at the bottom.

11 Lay a clean dish towel over the letters and the thick felt strip and press the letters into position, using a hot iron.

7.

Don't cut the strips of the stencil too finely or you risk them breaking.

10.

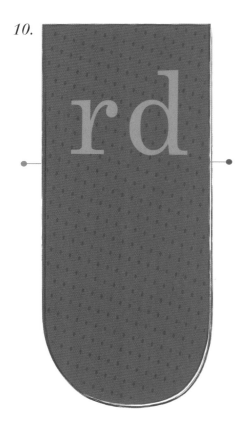

12 Thread your sewing machine with thread to match the craft felt and topstitch a neat line just inside the edge of the felt letters. (Turning the machine wheel by hand will give you more control when working around tight curves.)

13 Fold the case along the fold at the bottom, right side out, and pin down the side seams. Thread your sewing machine with the thread to match the thick felt and, starting from one bottom corner, topstitch all the way around the sides and the top of the flap, ³⁄₁₆ inch (5 mm) in from the outside edge. Make some additional stitches back and forth when you begin and end your stitching. Leave the fold at the bottom of the case unstitched.

14 Fold the flap over and make a mark on the front of the flap, centered on the width of the case. Using the topstitching thread, sew one of the buttons on at this point, just above the topstitching line. Then stitch the second button to the front of the case, positioning it so that it lies immediately below the first button when the flap is folded down.

15 Cut a 14-inch (36-cm) length of the waxed cord and tie a knot close to each end. Knot the cord around the top button on the case, about 2½ inches (6 cm) in from one end. Wrap the cord around the buttons in a figure-eight shape to hold the case shut.

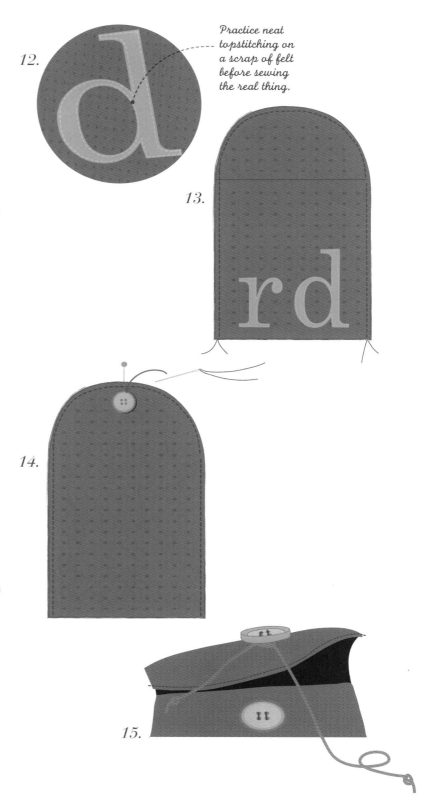

12.

Practice neat topstitching on a scrap of felt before sewing the real thing.

13.

14.

15.

{Lettered} Cushions

These cushions, with their gently shaded "OH," make a soft exclamation on your couch. You could add some punctuation on a third cushion (a question mark? An exclamation mark?) if you want them to have more emphasis. The examples in the photo are made from raw silk, but felt would also work well, and you could use bright or even neon colors to create a Pop-Art effect. The covers are made in an envelope pattern, so that it's easy to slip a cushion pad inside.

PERSONALIZING YOUR PROJECT

- Try a set of cushions in the same or toning fabrics but using letters from a variety of fonts.
- Eurostile's square characters are best used large on items such as towels or cushions.

ABOUT THE FONT

EUROSTILE BOLD

Developed at the Nebiolo type foundry in Turin, Italy, in 1962, Eurostile was an extension of an earlier, popular font, Microgramma.

FOR TWO CUSHIONS YOU WILL NEED

Templates on page 122

36 x 12 in. (91 x 31 cm) fusible web

Two 12-in. (31-cm) squares of gray felt

12-in. (31-cm) square of cream felt

18-in. (46-cm) square sheet of brown paper

20-in. (51-cm) piece each of two colors of raw silk (we used dusty pink and pale green), 45 in. (115 cm) wide

Two 18-in. (46-cm) square cushion pads

Sewing thread in gray, cream, pink and green

Sharp scissors

Pencil

Pair of compasses

Chalk pencil or tailor's chalk

Metal ruler

Straight pins

f a b c
f R M
G o *

Developed when much type design was deliberately "modern" in feel, Eurostile's square capitals with their slightly rounded corners looked typically fresh and slightly futuristic.

Making the cushions

1 Photocopy or scan the templates on page 122, enlarging them to scale, then print and cut them out.

2 Cut the shadows away from the letters, so that you have three pieces for the "O" (one letter piece and two shadows) and four pieces for the "H" (one letter piece and three shadows).

3 Cut the fusible web into three 12-inch (31-cm) squares. Following the manufacturer's instructions, apply one piece to the back of each of the three felt squares.

4 Place the main letter templates, reversed, on the fusible web side of the gray felt squares, one letter on each of the squares. Draw around the templates and cut the letter shapes out.

5 Place all the shadow templates, reversed, on the fusible web side of the cream felt square. Draw around the templates and cut the shadow shapes out.

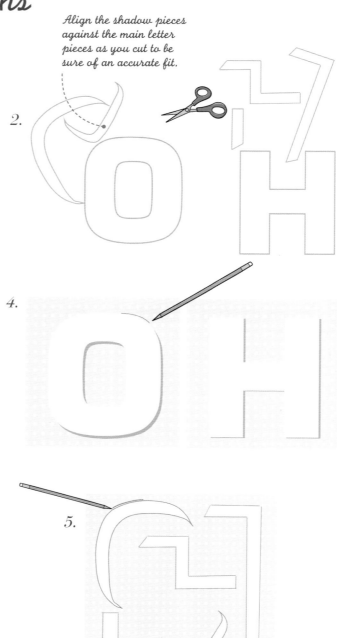

Align the shadow pieces against the main letter pieces as you cut to be sure of an accurate fit.

2.

4.

5.

6 Fold the brown paper square diagonally in both directions and crease sharply, then unfold, so that there is a fold line leading to each corner.

7 Use the ruler to set the pair of compasses to 3 inches (7.5 cm) and place the point about 4¼ inches (11 cm) up the fold line away from the corner, then draw a rounded corner. Repeat on the other three corners and cut the paper so that you have a square shape with rounded corners.

8 Fold the pattern in half vertically and horizontally and crease sharply, then unfold.

9 To make the pink "O" cushion, mark the pink silk with a centered horizontal line and a centered vertical line, using a chalk pencil lightly on the right side of the fabric.

10 Peel off the backing paper from the gray felt "O" piece and position it on the front of the pink silk in the center, using a ruler and the chalk lines to make sure that it's accurately placed. Cover with a clean dish towel and press with a warm iron.

11 Peel off the backing paper from the two cream felt shadow pieces and put them in place alongside the letter. Cover with a clean dish towel and press with a warm iron.

6.

9.
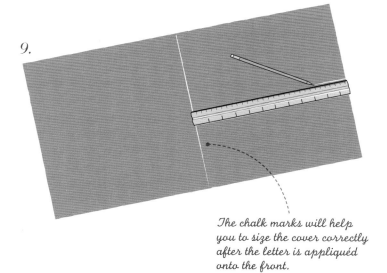

The chalk marks will help you to size the cover correctly after the letter is appliquéd onto the front.

10.
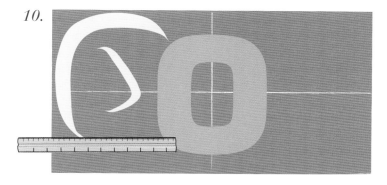

12 Thread the sewing machine with gray thread and zigzag stitch around the inside and outside edges of the "O." Rethread the machine with cream thread and zigzag stitch around the inside and outside edges of the cream shadow pieces.

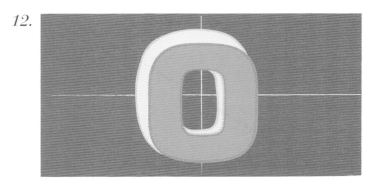

12.

13 Lay the fabric face down on your work surface and add horizontal and vertical lines with a chalk pencil as you did in step 9. Place the brown-paper pattern on top of it, aligning the horizontal and vertical folds with the chalk lines.

14 Draw around the paper pattern with a chalk pencil. This will ensure that the letter is in the center of the cushion.

Place the pattern exactly centered, using the chalk lines you drew earlier.

14.

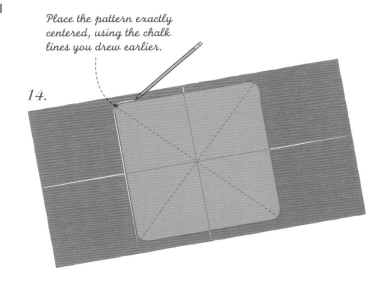

15 Fold under the selvage edges at the sides of the fabric once to the wrong side. Thread the sewing machine with pink thread and stitch the edges down.

16 Lay the fabric right side up on your work surface and fold the left-hand side of the fabric over to the center, folding it along the chalk-marked pattern edge.

15.

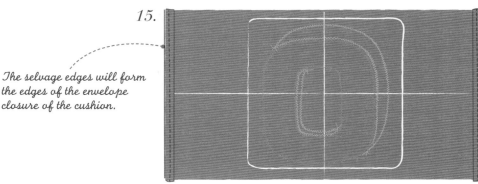

The selvage edges will form the edges of the envelope closure of the cushion.

17 Repeat with the right-hand side of the fabric so that the edge overlaps the left-hand edge. Pin around the open edges of the fabric, going through all the layers.

18 Turn the cover over, so that you can see the chalk outline of the cushion pattern. Using matching thread in the machine, sew the cover closed along the top and bottom, going around the curves on the corners. There is no need to stitch the straight sides, because these are on the folds of the fabric.

19 Trim the seam allowances along the top and bottom to ⅜ inch (1 cm). Zigzag stitch around the raw edges of the seam allowances. Turn the cushion cover right way out and press, then insert a cushion pad.

20 To make the second cover, repeat steps 9–19, using the felt and fabric for the "H" cushion.

17.

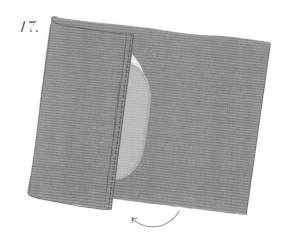

18.

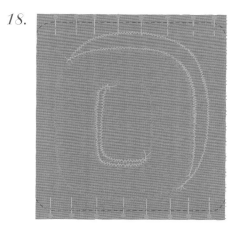

19.

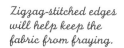

Zigzag-stitched edges will help keep the fabric from fraying.

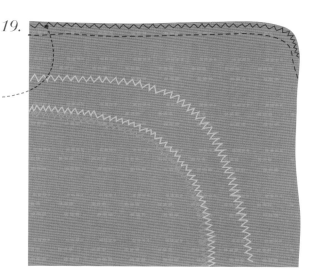

Your beloved pet deserves the best—and his own initial on his own jacket (in, perhaps, your or his favorite font) reflects that. This is simply worked as an appliqué patch that can be neatly stitched to any dog coat. Our instructions are for a medium-size patch, but if your pet weighs in at either end of the size spectrum (huge or tiny), you can scale the size of the circle and letter up or down to suit.

PERSONALIZING YOUR PROJECT

- Cooper Black doesn't have any fine points or thin strokes, so it can be adapted to any project that uses stencils and fabric paint.
- You could try overlapping letters in different colors for a different look.

ABOUT THE FONT

Cooper Black

Designed in the 1920s by Oswald Bruce Cooper of Chicago, Cooper Black has hefty outlines combined with relatively modest serifs—a classic display face. It was originally advertised as being for "far-sighted printers with near-sighted customers."

YOU WILL NEED

Dog coat or sweater with a plain back
6-in. (15-cm) square of fusible web
6-in. (15cm) square of red fleece fabric
10-in. (25.5-cm) square of cream flannel sheeting
10-in. (25.5-cm) square of heat-resistant batting
7¾-in. (19-cm)-diameter circle of thin cardboard
Red and cream sewing threads
Embroidery needle
Pencil
Fabric marking pen
Sharp scissors
Straight pins

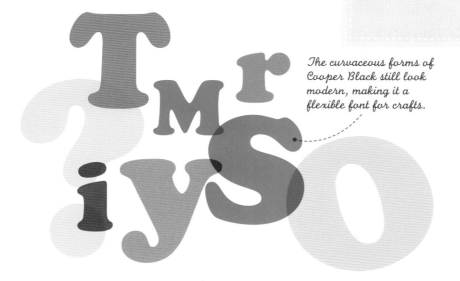

The curvaceous forms of Cooper Black still look modern, making it a flexible font for crafts.

Making the dog sweater

1 Print out your chosen letter at a size where it is no taller or wider than 4¾ inches (12 cm) and cut it out.

2 Following the manufacturer's instructions, press the fusible web onto the wrong side of the fleece fabric.

3 Reverse your letter template and lay it on the wrong side of the fleece. Pin it in place and draw around it with a pencil, then remove the pins and carefully cut it out.

4 Turn the letter right side up. Peel off the backing paper from the fusible web and iron the fleece letter diagonally onto the center of the piece of flannel sheeting.

5 Place the flannel sheeting on top of the batting, align the edges, and pin the layers together. Thread the sewing machine with red thread and work carefully around the edge of the letter, using a wide satin stitch. You may find it easier to turn the wheel by hand to keep control of the stitching around the details of the letter.

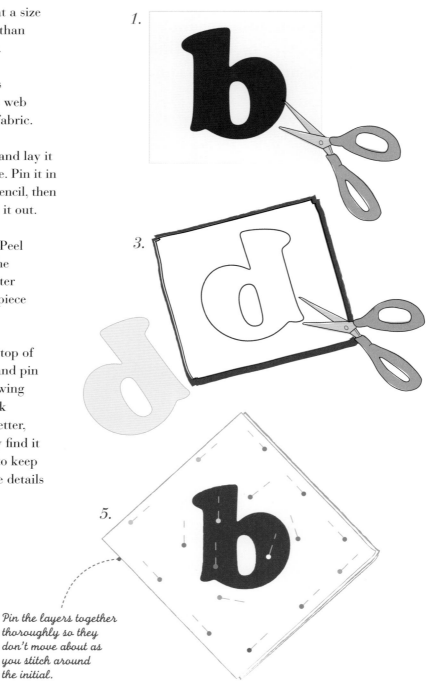

1.

3.

5.

Pin the layers together thoroughly so they don't move about as you stitch around the initial.

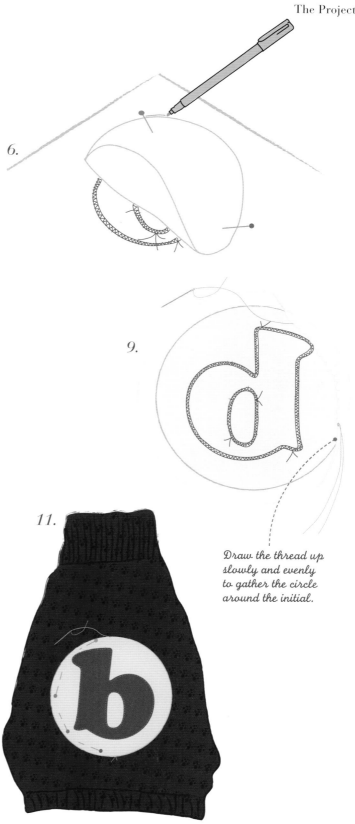

6. Turn the flannel square face down and carefully position the thin cardboard circle over the letter, making sure the letter is centered in the circle. Draw around the circle onto the batting with a fabric marking pen.

7. Carefully cut around the drawn circle, cutting out only the batting layer.

8. Draw a line around the edge of the cutout circle, ⅝ inch (1.5 cm) beyond the edge, and cut around the flannel layer.

9. Thread an embroidery needle with a double strand of cream thread and work a small running stitch by hand ¼ inch (6 mm) in from the raw edge of the flannel. When you've sewn all the way around, pull the threads to gather the edge of the flannel, so that the gathered edge lies on the back of the patch. Knot the thread.

10. Thread a needle with a single strand of cream thread and hand stitch the edge of the flannel down to the back of the batting near the edge to keep your patch flat, being careful not to stitch through to the front of the patch.

11. Pin the patch right way up to the center back of the dog coat. Using cream thread and a small ladder stitch, sew the patch onto the coat.

Draw the thread up slowly and evenly to gather the circle around the initial.

This stylish toiletry bag made from waterproof fabric uses red and blue on white for a crisp color combination. This clean design features a stylized showerhead plus the Spanish word for "bath," but you can use a different word or language. However, it's best to use a short word because the smaller the letters get, the more difficult it will be to cut them out neatly. We've suggested that you use a laminating machine to make the pattern—they're inexpensive and help you get an ultra-neat finish—but you can make the bag without one, using thin cardboard to make the stencil instead.

PERSONALIZING YOUR PROJECT

- You could make a set, with a bag in a different color for each member of the family.
- You can experiment with heavier waterproof fabrics for larger, outdoor projects.

ABOUT THE FONT
FUTURA MEDIUM

Balanced and functional, Futura is the best-known face designed by Paul Renner, a German typographer. He intended it to be workable across a wide range of applications and it is still a popular choice for everything from signage to book design.

YOU WILL NEED

Pattern on page 122
Laminating machine and laminating pouch
(or you can print or trace the pattern
on to thin cardboard)
9 x 3 in. (23 x 7.5 cm) red leatherette fabric
5 x 5 in. (13 x 13 cm) blue leatherette fabric
24 x 12 in. (61 x 31 cm) waterproof nursery
sheet; it has a rubber coating on one side and
a woven fabric on the other
12-in. (31-cm) white zipper with a closed end
Blue, red, and white sewing thread
Craft knife
Sharp scissors
Cutting mat
Ball-point pen
Pencil
High-tack craft glue
Metal ruler
Straight pins

Futura is a moderate face, based on symmetry.

Making the toiletry bag

1 Photocopy or scan the template on page 122, enlarging it to scale, then print and cut it out. Either copy it onto thin cardboard to use as a template or put your paper through a laminating machine in a glued pouch.

2 Cut out the showerhead, the water drops, and the lettering, leaving some small strips connecting the middle sections of the "B", the "A", and the "O", so that the centers stay in place.

3 Turn the stencil over (so the letters read in reverse), and use a ball-point pen to mark out the letters on the back of the red leatherette. Cut the letters out carefully, using a craft knife and a metal ruler on a cutting mat.

4 Repeat the process with the showerhead and water drops pattern, using the blue leatherette.

1.

2.

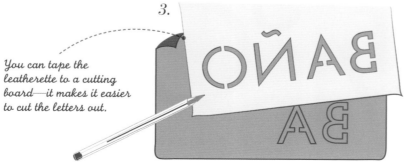

3.

You can tape the leatherette to a cutting board—it makes it easier to cut the letters out.

5 Lay out the rectangle of nursery sheet and mark the middle of the upper 12-inch (31-cm) edge with a pencil. Place the stencil on the sheet, centering it so that the top of the showerhead is aligned with the edge of the fabric and is in the middle of the strip. Use a pencil to mark some points at the corners and along the edges of the letters, the showerhead shape, and the water drops.

6 Remove the stencil and use high-tack craft glue to stick the leatherette pieces in place, using the guide marks you have made. Let dry. (If you put the fabric under a pile of glossy magazines, it will help the letters stick evenly to get the best result.)

7 Thread your sewing machine with blue thread and stitch neatly just inside the edges of the showerhead pattern and the drops. Rethread the machine with red thread and repeat, this time stitching inside the edges of the letters.

5.

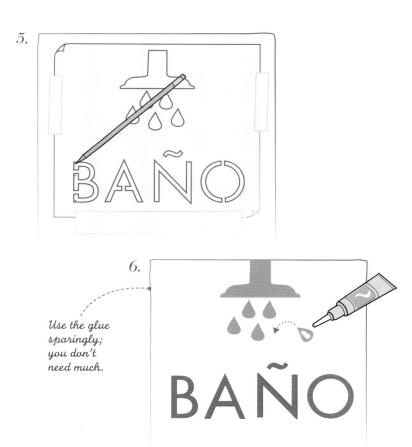

6.

Use the glue sparingly; you don't need much.

7.

It may be easier to turn the wheel of the machine by hand when you are outlining small areas.

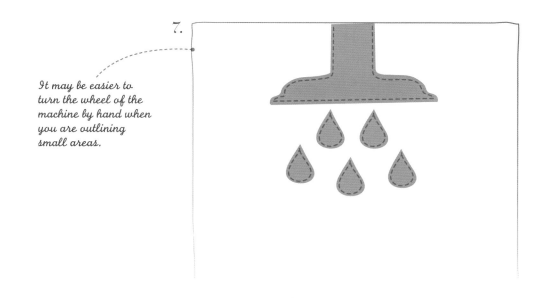

8 Pin the zipper along the top edge of the rectangle, with the right side of the zipper facing the right side of the fabric. Thread the sewing machine with white thread and stitch a line through the zipper and fabric, ¼ inch (6 mm) down from the top edge, reverse stitching for 1 inch (2.5 cm) at the start and the finish.

9 Fold the fabric over, right sides together, and pin the other side of the zipper along the opposite short edge of the fabric. Stitch again. You will now have a tube of fabric, joined by the zipper.

10 Turn the bag right side out and undo the zipper. Fold the fabric back down away from the zipper edge. Pin the fabric down and stitch along both sides of the zipper again.

Practice machine stitching on a scrap of waterproof fabric to get the tension even before you sew the zipper in place.

11 Close the zipper again and turn the bag inside out, keeping the zipper pull inside the bag. Pin the open sides together, folding the bag so that the zipper falls 1 inch (2.5 cm) down from the top edge. Using white thread, stitch down both sides of the bag, ¼ inch (6 mm) in from the edges of the fabric, stitching over the zipper and reverse stitching at the start and finish.

12 Trim off the excess zipper tape flush with the fabric edge, and use a small line of zigzag machine stitch to stop it from fraying.

13 To make the lower corners and give the toiletry bag a flat bottom, flatten out the lower corner of one of the seamed sides of the bag, as shown, so that the seam is on top of the fold. Pin it flat, then take a ruler and mark with a pencil a line 2½ inches (6 cm) long at 90 degrees to the seam.

14 Stitch along the line, reverse stitching at the start and finish, then cut off the corner ¼ inch (6 mm) below the stitching. Repeat steps 13 and 14 with the second corner, then turn the bag right side out.

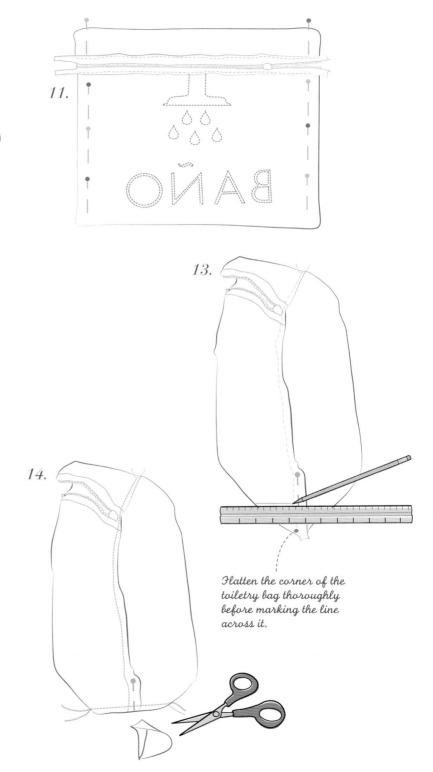

11.

13.

14.

Flatten the corner of the toiletry bag thoroughly before marking the line across it.

{One-Letter} Doorstop

Made from hard-wearing canvas, weighted with dried beans and adorned with a single bold and cheerful two-tone letter, this doorstop would make a terrific housewarming gift. It's quick to make, and the two-color treatment of a single letter makes a strong visual impact. The template is for a letter that narrows at the top slightly—you will need to adjust it if the letter you choose to use is a significantly different shape, such as a "W," which will require a wider, more square shape.

PERSONALIZING YOUR PROJECT

- Dividing single letters into colored halves can work well with any font, provided that the font is both bold and simple enough to take it.

ABOUT THE FONT

BERNARD MT CONDENSED

Bold and chunky, Bernard looks as though it might be a product of the 1960s, so it's a surprise to learn that it was first issued commercially in 1926. You can see its origins in some of the blocky advertising fonts of the late nineteenth century; it's readable, but still has plenty of personality.

ag ek
or

Lowercase characters in Bernard have some surprisingly narrow strokes, so they're a little more challenging to cut neatly.

YOU WILL NEED

Templates on page 120–1

1-yd. (1-m) length mid-weight cream canvas fabric

12-in. (31-cm) square turquoise felt

12-in. (31-cm) square dark blue felt

12-in. (31-cm) square fusible web

12 in. (31 cm) striped or checkered ribbon, 1 in. (2.5 cm) wide

Bag polyester fiber filling

5 cups (2¼ lb./1 kg) dried rice

Tacking thread

Cream sewing thread

Sewing needle

Sharp scissors

Fabric marking pen

Pencil

High-tack craft glue

Metal ruler

Straight pins

Making the doorstop

1 Print out your chosen letter at 9 inches (23 cm) high. Select the appropriate pattern pieces on pages 120–1 for the size and shape of your letter, then photocopy or scan them, enlarge to scale, and print them out.

2 Cut roughly around the paper template (at this stage, you don't need to cut out any internal space, such as the center of the "A"). Using a ruler, draw a pencil line across the back of the template exactly halfway up the letter.

3 Next, cut out the pattern pieces to make the body of the doorstop and pin them onto the canvas. Cut around them, leaving a 1-inch (2.5-cm) seam allowance around each of the pieces.

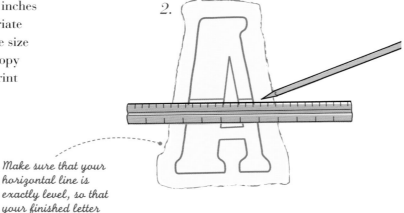

2.

Make sure that your horizontal line is exactly level, so that your finished letter will look balanced.

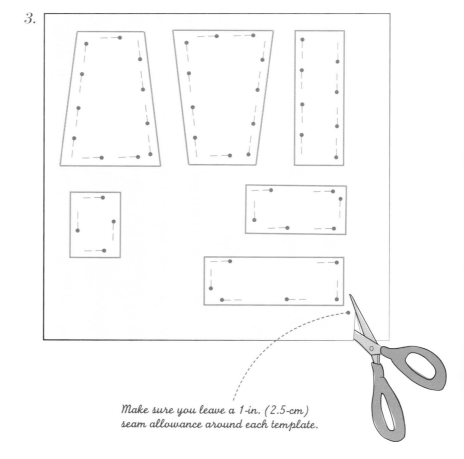

3.

Make sure you leave a 1-in. (2.5-cm) seam allowance around each template.

4 Lay out your two felt pieces, aligning them together along a horizontal axis. Place the fusible web on top of them, with the bonding agent facing down and the peel-off backing facing up. Finally, put the letter template wrong side up on top, precisely aligning the center pencil line along the line where the two colors of felt meet. Use tiny dots of high-tack craft glue in the corners of the paper template to hold it in place on top of the fusible web.

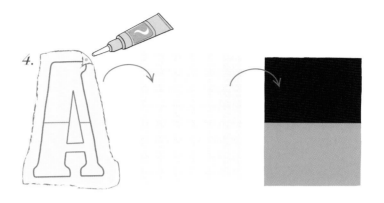

5 Cover with a clean dish towel and press with a warm iron.

6 Now carefully cut the letter out of the felt, using scissors.

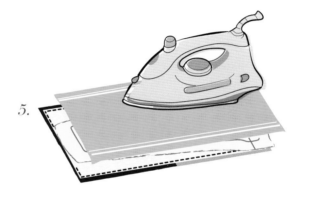

7 Lay the letter right side up on the front canvas panel of your doorstop. Use a ruler to place it centered, then make small marks around the edges of the letter with a fabric marking pen, so that you can reposition it accurately. Peel off the backing paper from the fusible web and carefully position the letter on the canvas, following your marks. Place a clean cloth over the felt, then press in place with a medium-hot iron.

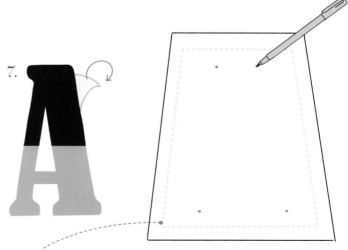

The pencil guides will help you to place the letters accurately.

8 With the wrong sides facing out, pin and tack together the short sides of the bottom and side pieces of your doorstop, then thread your sewing machine with the cream thread and sew the three pieces into a strip, using a 1-inch (2.5-cm) seam allowance. Press the seams open. Pin and tack the front and back pieces in place, easing the sides into place to fit, so that you have an open-topped bag, then machine stitch, again using a 1-inch (2.5-cm) seam allowance. Press the seams open and trim the corners.

9 Pin the ribbon to the sides of the top piece of the doorstop, then tack the top in place along both sides and the front, leaving the back top edge open. Machine stitch the seams, then turn the doorstop right side out.

10 Pad the bottom of the doorstop with a thin layer of polyester fiber filling to a depth of about 2 inches (5 cm), then pour in the rice to weigh the doorstop. When all the rice has been added, shake the doorstop so that it's weighted evenly, then add pieces of polyester fiber filling until the whole doorstop is firmly padded.

11 Turn under the raw edges of the last open seam, thread a sewing needle with cream thread, and slip stitch the gap closed.

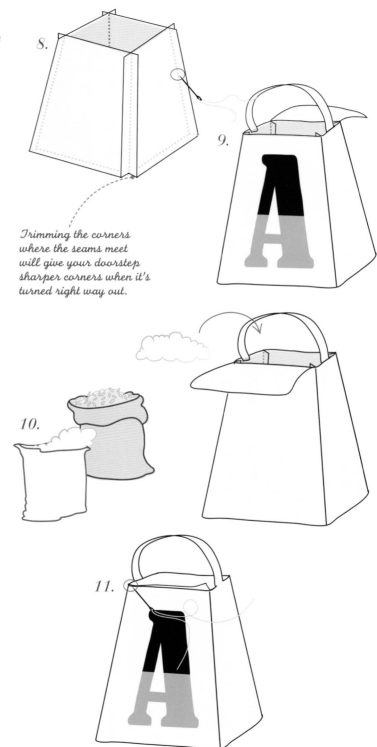

8.

Trimming the corners where the seams meet will give your doorstep sharper corners when it's turned right way out.

9.

10.

11.

Old-fashioned café blinds were originally designed to provide a little privacy behind a window opening out onto the street, but without blocking out light. Our version is made from light linen and muslin, so the blind, hung from an elastic from the halfway point on the window, remains translucent. Our blind is about one yard square; you may need to adjust the sizes of the muslin and linen, depending on the size of your window.

PERSONALIZING YOUR PROJECT

- Calligraphic fonts make for gorgeous results, but take your time planning their use—they call for a sharp and immaculate finish.

ABOUT THE FONT

Bickham Script

Inspired by an eighteenth-century manual, *The Universal Penman*, and named for its author, George Bickham, this font was, in fact, created in the late 1990s by the American typographer Richard Lipton. Beautiful and showy, it's best used in small doses.

Lovely, but challenging: the lavish curlicues of Bickham call for a steady hand as you work.

YOU WILL NEED

Template on page 125

Two 48 x 10-in. (121 x 25.5-cm) strips natural muslin fabric

48 x 25 in. (121 x 63 cm) beige linen fabric

Two sheets letter-format T-shirt transfer paper for light fabrics

Sewing thread in a natural color

Darning needle

Pencil

Masking tape

1-yd. (1-m) metal ruler

Straight pins

Making the blind

1 Lay the muslin strips on top of each side of the long edges of the linen, then pin them together. Thread the sewing machine with the thread in a natural color and sew the strips on each side of the linen, using a ½-inch (12-mm) seam allowance.

2 Press the two seams flat with a hot iron, pressing them toward the muslin edges of the blind.

3 Machine a second line of stitching ¼ inch (6 mm) into the seam allowance, along the pressed edges of the fabric.

4 Use the darning needle to pull out some threads along the raw edge of the fabric on the seam allowances to create a delicately frayed edge (the second row of stitching will prevent the fabric from fraying too far).

1.

Pull out the edge threads one at a time—it's easier than trying to remove several all at once.

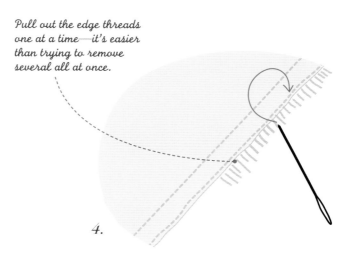

4.

5 Now, make a hem along the sides of the blind. Use the ruler and a pencil to mark a line 2 inches (5 cm) in from the long raw edges of the muslin, fold the raw edges up to the pencil lines and press, then fold the edges over again and press to create a 1-inch (2.5-cm) hem. Machine stitch along the hems on both sides of the blind.

6 Spread out your blind and, if necessary, trim the top edge to a straight line (muslin is an open fabric and can stretch a little as you work). Create a hem aross the top edge, folding and pressing as in the previous step.

7 Pin in place, then machine stitch a line of stitching close to the bottom edge of the turned top of the blind, securing with a few reverse stitches at the beginning and end of the seam. You now have an open channel at the top of the blind to hold the curtain wire.

8 Repeat steps 5 and 6 to create a hem at the bottom edge of the blind. Because the lower hem does not need to form a channel, stitch along the opening at each end of it to make a neat finish.

7.

8.

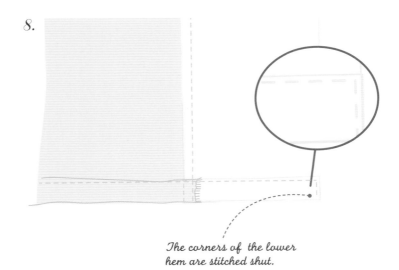

The corners of the lower hem are stitched shut.

9 Photocopy or scan the template for "Café" from page 125 and enlarge to scale. Following the manufacturer's instructions, print the word onto the transfer paper (remember, the word is reversed in order to appear the right way around on the blind). Depending on the size of the paper you are using, you may need to split the template into multiple sections before printing and rejoin them after printing them out.

10 Cut the lettering out, leaving about 1/16 to 1/8 inch (2 to 3 mm) around the edges—particularly around the narrowest parts of the characters. Butt the pieces of the word together and join them with strips of masking tape, cutting away any excess tape when the parts are joined.

11 Carefully position the lettering in the center of the linen strip on your blind, and use the ruler to check it is straight.

12 Iron the word in place, following the manufacturer's instructions, then carefully peel the backing off the transfer paper and hang your blind.

10.

11.

12.

As the transfer backing is peeled off, the colored lettering is revealed.

Fonts that play visual tricks are best used sparingly in fabric projects; after all, you still want to be able to make the letters out. These napkins, made with a simple stenciling technique, show off the elaborate "folds" of a modern alphabet that deliberately mimics origami forms.

PERSONALIZING YOUR PROJECT

- Novelty fonts that copy natural forms—from butterflies to bubbles and folded paper to wood grain—can be charming but still practical enough to use.

ABOUT THE FONT

ORIGAMI

A contemporary font created by the German designer Peter Fritzsche. Origami was originally based on folded strips of paper and looks convincingly three-dimensional. It's best used for initals rather than phrases, allowing you to enjoy its ingenious forms.

YOU WILL NEED

White cotton napkins

Letter-size sheets of white paper

Laminator and laminating pouches

Two 12-in. (31-cm) squares of corrugated cardboard

Craft knife

Ball-point pen

Five fine-tip fabric painting pens in fluorescent colors (you can buy these in packages)

Metal ruler

Straight pins

With a font as structurally complex as this one, you may prefer to stick to a single color to keep the characters clear-cut.

Making the table linen

1 Print out your chosen sets of initials (or single letters) 2 inches (5 cm) high. You'll be able to get several sets on a single sheet of paper. Leave a margin of 1 inch (2.5 cm) from the edge of the paper and 2 inches (5 cm) between each pair of letters.

2 Laminate the paper, using a laminator and a laminating pouch. Cut each set of initials into a separate rectangle, leaving a margin of at least 1 inch (2.5 cm) around the edge. Then, using the craft knife and ruler, cut out each set of initials to make the stencils.

3 Iron the napkins. Measure the depth of the hem on the napkins.

4 On each stencil, measure the hem's depth plus 1/16 inch (2 mm) down from the bottom of the letters. Draw a horizontal line parallel to the bottom of the letters at this point and cut off any excess to make the baseline of your stencil.

5 Measure from the outer edges of the letters on each of the stencils to find the center point and mark it with a ball-point pen.

1.

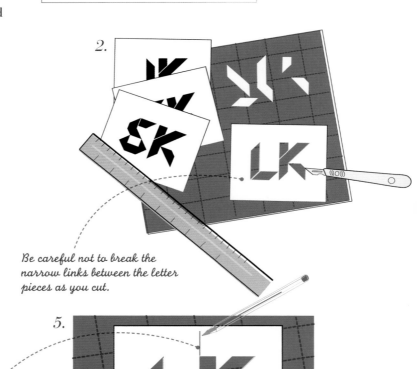

Be careful not to break the narrow links between the letter pieces as you cut.

The center point is halfway between the overall width of both the letters and the space between them.

6 Fold your napkins in half and mark the center point of one edge with a pin, then unfold your napkins.

7 Lay a double layer of corrugated cardboard on your work surface and add a couple of layers of plain white paper on top. Lay a napkin on top of the stack.

8 Line up the center marks on the stencil and napkin and use pins to hold the stencil in place. If you splay the pins outward from the letter spaces, you will find it easier to color in the letters.

9 Using a fine-point fabric pen, draw around the outline of each letter. Use the pen with a light touch—if you stop too long in the corners of the stencil, the ink from the pen will bleed into the fabric and the sharp corners of the letters will be lost. After completing the outlines, color the letters in using straight, even strokes.

10 Set the fabric ink with an iron, following the manufacturer's instructions. Repeat all the steps for each napkin, using a different fluorescent color for the initials on each one.

6.

8.

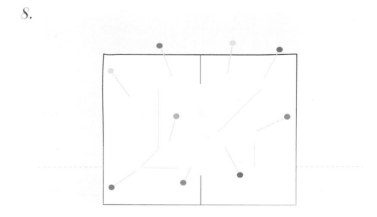

9.

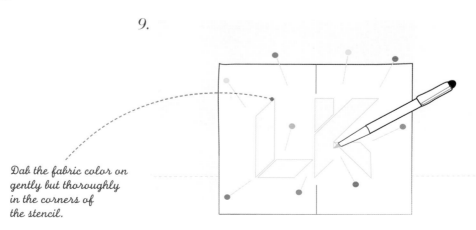

Dab the fabric color on gently but thoroughly in the corners of the stencil.

{Ampersand} Bookends

You can make matching ampersands for a pair of these bookends or use different letters—the only limit is that, to be functional, the characters you choose must have some weight at the bottom to balance the weight of the books. Arial is a practical, balanced font, so will work well here, as would other even sans-serif shapes, such as Gill Sans or Helvetica. The extra-thick felt can be found online if it isn't available in your local craft store.

PERSONALIZING YOUR PROJECT

- The thick felt cuts to make good sturdy font shapes, so you could experiment with larger letters to make items such as a child's play mat or a hanging storage pocket.

ABOUT THE FONT

Arial Bold

A modern font, first released to the market in 1982 by Monotype Typography, Arial has been described by one of the team who designed it, Robin Nicholas, as "a generic sans serif." Its outlines are neat and practical, and its slightly generic quality makes it endlessly flexible.

FOR EACH BOOKEND YOU WILL NEED

Template on page 121

31½ x 9¾ in. (80 x 25 cm) gray felt, ³⁄₁₆ in. (5 mm) thick

2-yd. (2-m) length of waxed cotton cord, ³⁄₁₆ in. (2 mm) in diameter (found online or in craft stores); we used pink

5 cups (2¼ lb./1 kg) dried lentils or small plastic toy-filling pellets

Small quantity of polyester fiber filling

Craft knife

Sharp scissors

Cutting mat

Hole punch

Black fine-tip felt pen

Latex contact adhesive

Craft glue

Glue spreader or small craft spatula

Metal ruler

Funnel or liquid measuring cup

Straight pins

Uppercase letters will work best for this project—"G," "C," "B," "D," or "U" would all be good picks.

Making the bookends

1 Photocopy or scan the template on page 121, enlarging it to scale, then print and cut it out. Use the smallest setting on the hole punch to punch the holes shown on the pattern.

2 Place the pattern on the gray felt and cut out the two flat sides of the ampersand. Position the pattern as economically as possible, because the strips to make the edges of the ampersand are cut from the remainder of the felt.

3 On the right side of one of the felt ampersands, mark all the holes through the pattern with the fine-tip pen and, using the smallest setting on the hole punch, punch them through. Leave the other side unmarked.

4 Using a metal ruler and a craft knife on a cutting mat, cut the remainder of the felt into strips 2 inches (5 cm) wide. Make sure that you keep the strips as long as possible—you will need at least one that is a minimum of 14½ inches (37 cm) long, so that you can use it to make the top of the ampersand with no seams.

1.

3.

4.

Arrange the felt so that you can cut as many long strips from the leftovers as possible.

5 To make the inner edges of the ampersand, start with the internal holes. Place the front (pierced) side wrong side up on a solid work surface and stand one of the 2-inch (5-cm) strips on its edge. Starting at the corner of the upper hole, curve the strip around the hole. Push pins through both pieces at an angle to hold the strip in place, pinning it around the hole, flush with the edge of the felt. Where the strip crosses back on itself at the bottom of the hole, make a mark with the fine-tip pen to show where the short end of the felt touches the inside surface of the strip.

6 Unpin the strip and cut it across at an exact right angle at the pen mark.

7 Use the glue spreader or spatula to scrape a ³/₁₆-inch (5-mm)-wide line of latex contact adhesive around the hole, going right to the edges. Then spread a thin layer of glue along one of the long edges of the strip.

8 Let the glue dry completely, or speed it up with a hair dryer. The glue should turn completely transparent before you secure it (it's opaque when still damp).

5.

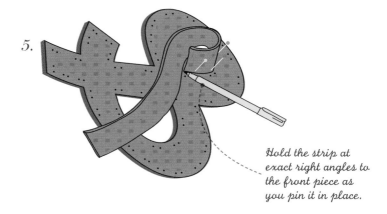

Hold the strip at exact right angles to the front piece as you pin it in place.

6.

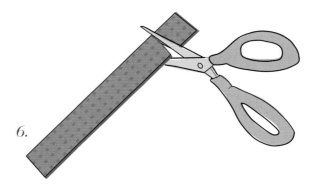

The layer of glue on both pieces should be spread thinly.

7.

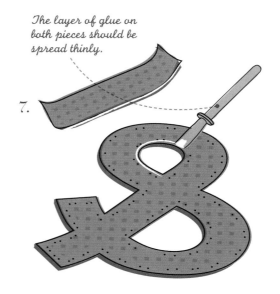

9 Position the strip around the hole on the front piece. Pinch along the seam really hard between your thumb and first two fingers to make sure it sticks securely.

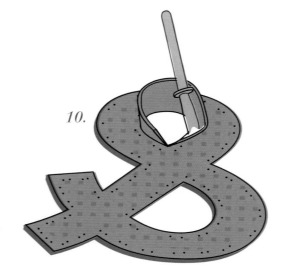

10.

10 Spread a thin layer on one end of the felt strip across the thickness of the felt itself and another thin layer on the inner edge of the other end. Let dry as before and, when opaque, pinch the edges together firmly along the seam.

11 Repeat the process with another strip of felt around the second hole in the front piece.

12 Now glue strips around the outside of the ampersand front, using the same technique. The diagram shows you how the strips should fit together. Use the longest strip around the top of the ampersand front, so that your finished bookend will have a smooth top, without seams.

Look at the circled seams of the felt strips on the right and follow them to make the sides of the ampersand.

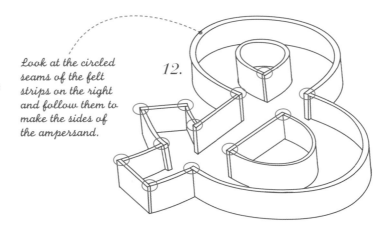

12.

13 Thread the pink cord through the prepunched holes in the front in a running-stitch pattern, using one piece around each of the internal holes and one piece around the outer edge. At the end of each stitching round, tie the two cord ends together, cut the ends to ¾ inch (2 cm) and use craft glue on the ends to make sure that they won't come undone.

13.

14 Place the ampersand face down on your work surface. Mark a gap at the top with pins to make sure that you leave a gap for the filling as you glue the shape together.

15 As before, apply a fine line of latex contact adhesive around the edge of the back piece and along the edges of the strips that form the gusset of the ampersand. Let dry, then position the back piece over the glued edges and pinch firmly all along the ampersand's outer edge to secure.

16 Using a funnel or liquid measuring cup, fill the ampersand through the gap at the top with the lentils or plastic toy pellets. Fill the shape about up to the halfway point, where the upper and lower loops meet. Fill the balance with polyester fiber filling, pushing small quantities into the gap until the ampersand is solidly filled.

17 Glue along the sides of the gap, using latex contact adhesive. Let dry, then align the sides of the opening and firmly pinch closed, as before.

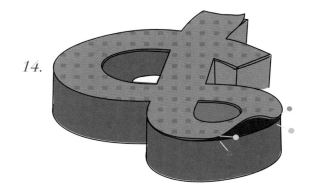

14.

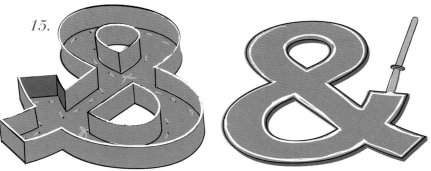

15.

16.

Push in wisps of stuffing, a little at a time, to fill the shape completely.

Y ou can't have too many potholders, and these usefully spell out the warning "Hot" in French and German as well as English. They're easy to make—the letters are simply machine-stitched outlines filled in with colored zigzag stitching. The sturdy black denim is washable, and these will keep looking fresh however tough their kitchen duty.

PERSONALIZING YOUR PROJECT

* Once you've mastered the art of creating a letter outline on the sewing machine and then filling it in with zigzagging stiches, it can be a good way of reproducing some of the more complex/difficult fonts on any textile, from denim to poplin.

ABOUT THE FONT

Seebad

Created by the Swiss designer Silvan Kaeser, and launched commercially in 2003, Seebad was allegedly inspired by some signage seen along the shore of Lake Geneva.

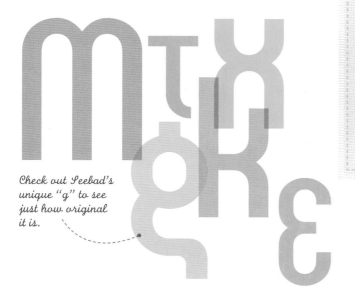

Check out Seebad's unique "g" to see just how original it is.

FOR THREE POTHOLDERS YOU WILL NEED

Templates on page 123

Thin cardboard to print on (or a laminating machine and laminating pouches)

30 x 20 in. (76 x 51 cm) black denim

Three 10-in. (25.5-cm) squares firm iron-on fusible interfacing

Three 10-in. (25.5-cm) squares heat-resistant batting

Six 100-yd. (100-m) reels sewing thread, two in bright pink, two in fluorescent yellow, and two in orange

Black sewing thread

60 in. (152 cm) bias tape, 1 in. (2.5 cm) wide each in bright pink, bright yellow, and bright orange

Craft knife

Sharp scissors

Cutting mat

White gel craft pen

Metal ruler

Pair of compasses

Straight pins

Making the potholders

1 Cut a square measuring 9 x 9 inches (23 x 23 cm) from a sheet of paper. Fold it diagonally in both directions and crease sharply, then unfold so that there is a fold line leading to each corner.

2 Use the ruler to set the compasses to 1½ inches (4 cm) and place the point about 2⅛ inches (5.4 cm) up and away from a corner and draw a rounded corner. Repeat on two of the other corners and cut around the lines, so that the paper square has three rounded corners and one squared corner.

3 Photocopy or scan the templates on page 123, enlarging them to scale, then print and cut them out. Either copy them onto thin cardboard to use as templates or put your paper through a laminating machine in laminating pouches.

4 Use the craft knife and metal ruler on a cutting mat to cut out the words to form a stencil. Where the letters have centers, leave small tabs of cardboard to hold them in place.

1.

2.

4.

The tabs are just to hold the centers of the letters in place—you will fill them in when you start stitching.

5 Cut six 10-inch (25.5-cm) squares from the black denim. Use a hot iron to press a square of interfacing onto the backs of three of them.

6 Use the gel pen to draw around the paper pattern on one of the pieces of interfaced denim, then position the first word stencil within the outline as shown and draw in the outlines of the letters. Repeat with the second and third word stencils.

7 Thread the sewing machine with the bright yellow thread and stitch carefully around the outlines of the letters of "CHAUD!," including the exclamation mark. When you've completed the outlines once, sew around them a second time; you may find it easier to turn the machine by hand to keep the stitching exactly on the lines as you go around the curves.

8 Switch the machine's setting to zigzag and practice on a scrap of denim to find the width of stitch you will need to fill in your letters with two or three rows of zigzag stitch. The words "CHAUD!" and "HEIß!" can be filled with two rows; "HOT!" is larger, so will need three rows to fill. Carefully stitch within the letters for "CHAUD!" until they are completely filled in. To fill in the dot at the bottom of the exclamation mark, you'll find it easier to combine zigzag with running stitch. Repeat the same process for the other two holders, using a different color of thread for each.

6.

7.

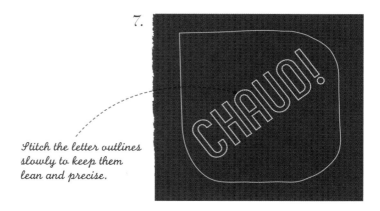

Stitch the letter outlines slowly to keep them lean and precise.

8.

9.

9 Cut around the pattern outline for all three pieces of embroidered denim. Cut out the three remaining pieces for the backs of the potholders, too, remembering to reverse the pattern.

10 Draw around the pattern three times on the squares of heat-resistant batting and cut them out.

11 Place a plain denim back right side down on your work surface, with a piece of batting and the "Chaud!" front right side up on top, aligning the edges, and pin all three layers together.

12 Thread the machine with pink thread and, using a large running stitch, sew around the potholder, stitching through all three layers ¼ inch (6 mm) in from the edge. Remove the pins.

13 Open out one side of the pink bias binding and, starting at the nonrounded corner, pin it around the edge of the potholder, flush with the edge. Place the pins at 90 degrees to the edge—this means that you can stitch straight over them. Leave the excess binding on at the end; this will form the hanging loop.

11.

13.

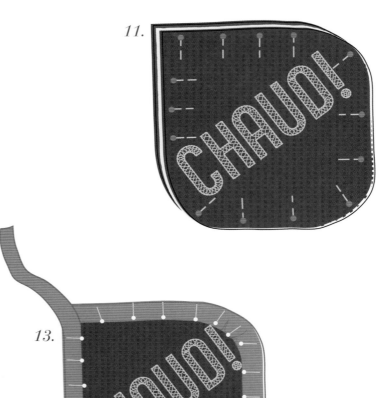

Take in the extra fullness on the corners as you pin the tape on.

14 Turn the potholder over, fold the loose edge of the bias binding over to the back, and pin in place.

15 Place the potholder front facing upward in the machine, and stitch around the edge of the bias binding, going through all three layers. When you get to the top left-hand corner, continue to stitch the excess length of binding in half.

16 Use the excess binding to make a 2-inch (5-cm) loop, and tuck the raw end over at the back of the potholder, on top of the bias strip. Stitch back and forth on the machine to secure along the previous line of stitching on the binding. Finish off the thread.

17 Repeat steps 11–16 to complete the other two potholders. Use contrasting colors for letters and tape for each, following the photograph.

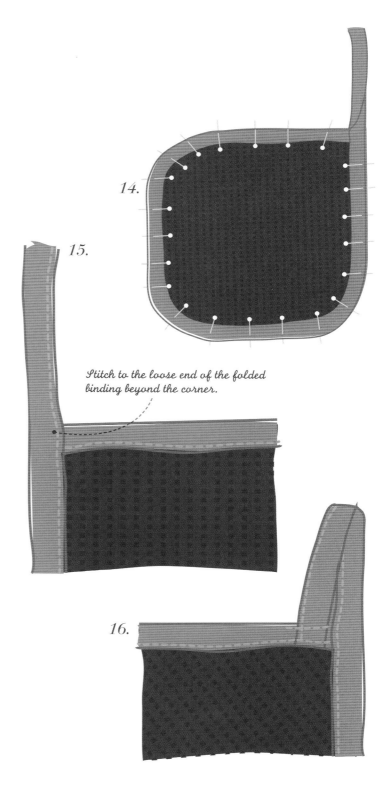

14.

15.

Stitch to the loose end of the folded binding beyond the corner.

16.

This cell phone case uses Rosewood, an elaborate font that works best in limited quantities. A single initial—and particularly one that lights up in its translucent window when the phone rings—is a perfect application for it. Choose brightly contrasting shades for the letter and the case for the best effect.

PERSONALIZING YOUR PROJECT

- Dramatic fonts, such as Rosewood, offer you the potential for two-color letters.
- While we have printed the font onto paper, it can also work well as a crisp appliqué, either in felt or a lighter, but still nonfray, fabric.

ABOUT THE FONT

Although it was only released by Adobe in 1994, Rosewood, designed by Carol Twombly, Carl Crossgrove, and Kim Buker Chansler, was inspired by Clarendon Ornamented, a complex display font widely used in the 1880s.

YOU WILL NEED

Lletter-size sheet of craft foam, ¹⁄₁₆ in. (2 mm) thick

Sheet of tracing paper that is suitable for use with your printer

Laminating machine and laminating pouch

Sewing thread to match the foam

20-in. (51-cm) length of cotton tape, ³⁄₈ in. (1 cm) wide, to match the foam

Craft knife

Pencil

Masking tape

Double-sided tape, ⁵⁄₁₆ in. (8 mm) wide

Cloth tape measure

Metal ruler

Straight pins

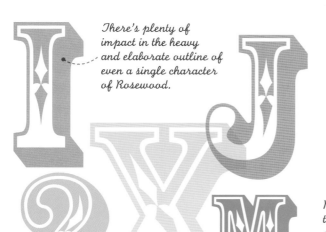

There's plenty of impact in the heavy and elaborate outline of even a single character of Rosewood.

Rosewood is what's technically known as a chromatic, or multicolored, font.

Making the cell phone case

1 Use the cloth tape measure to measure around your cell phone both width- and lengthwise. Make sure you take the measurements precisely, without any slack in the tape measure.

2 Halve the width measurement and add ½ in. (12 mm) in total for the seam allowances. Using the metal ruler and the craft knife, cut a strip this width from the craft foam, then trim it to the length measurement.

3 Size your initial letter so that it is 1½ inches (4 cm) narrower than the width of your foam strip. Print it in color on your tracing paper (if you don't have a color printer, a print shop can do this for you). Cut it out, leaving ¼ inch (6 mm) all around the letter. Cut a second piece of tracing paper the same size.

4 Align the plain piece of tracing paper behind the lettered piece, place them in the top of the laminator pouch, then laminate them in the machine.

5 Cut the letter out, leaving ¹⁄₁₆ inch (2 mm) all around the edge of the paper.

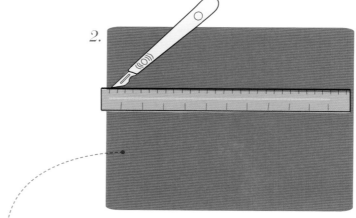

2.

If this is your first time working with craft foam or laminated paper, it's worth practicing cutting and sewing with them before starting on the project itself.

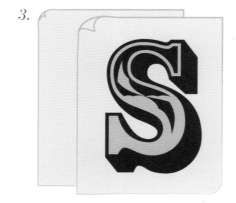

3.

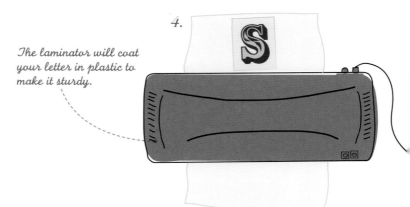

4.

The laminator will coat your letter in plastic to make it sturdy.

6 Using the letter as a template, cut a window in the center of a letter-size sheet of paper. The window needs to be slightly smaller than the tracing paper, so that it overlaps the edges of the letter piece a little.

7 Draw a line lightly in pencil across the width of your foam piece halfway down the long sides. Draw a second line across the width of your foam halfway between the top edge and the first line. Draw a third line from the center of the top edge down to the center of the first line.

8 Fold the paper window pattern in half both lengthwise and widthwise. Lay it over the foam, with the lengthwise and widthwise folds aligning with the second and third pencil lines on the foam respectively.

9 Mark the corners of the window on the foam with pencil, join the lines with a ruler, and use a ruler and a craft knife to cut the window out of the foam.

10 Position your letter behind the window and secure it in place right on the edge of the window with masking tape, leaving about a ⅛ inch (4 mm) gap all around uncovered, where the window overlaps the foam (this is where the letter will be stitched to the foam), and then adding more tape to the center of the letter.

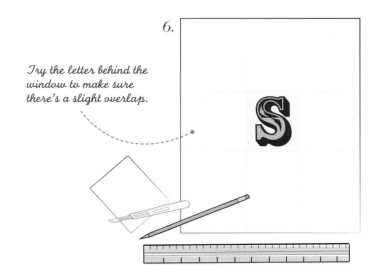

6.

Try the letter behind the window to make sure there's a slight overlap.

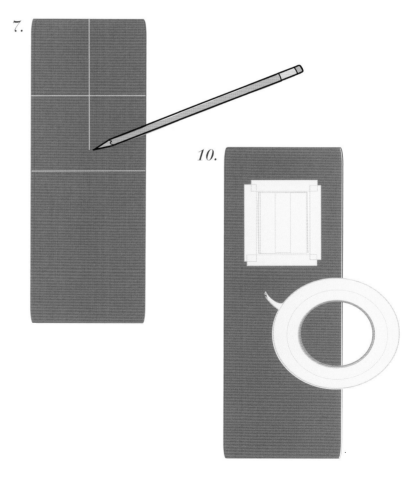

7.

10.

11 Thread the sewing machine with matching thread. With the front of the letter facing upward in the machine, slowly stitch around the edge of the window, stitching 1/16 inch (2 mm) from the edge.

12 Peel the masking tape off the back of the window. Pull the threads through to the wrong side of the foam and tie them off, then use a needle to stitch the ends into the machine stitches to secure.

13 Cut the length of cotton tape in half. Use pins to hold one half taut on a piece of corrugated cardboard or a craft workboard and apply a length of double-sided tape along it.

14 Peel off the backing paper from the double-sided tape, then unpin the cotton tape and secure it along the top edge of the foam strip, leaving a short length overhanging at the right-hand edge.

12.

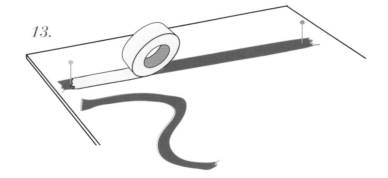

Practice stitching on a scrap of foam before sewing around the frame—turn the wheel manually and set the machine to a long stitch.

13.

14.

15 Turn the foam strip over so that the wrong side is facing upward, fold the short overhanging length over the edge and secure it down, then align and secure the long remaining piece of tape along the back top edge. Trim the end of the tape at the edge of the foam.

16 Repeat steps 14 and 15 to bind the lower end of the foam strip with the second length of cotton tape in the same way.

17 With the foam strip right side up in the sewing machine and using a long stitch and sewing slowly, as before, sew around the taped ends of the foam. When you've finished, knot the threads and sew the ends into the edge of the tape by hand.

18 Fold the foam strip in half to make the case. Pin the cotton tapes at the top together. Carefully machine stitch down the sides, 1/16 in. (2 mm) in from the edges, reverse stitching at the start and finish of each seam to secure. Knot the threads, stitch them to the inside of the case by hand, and cut the ends off.

17.

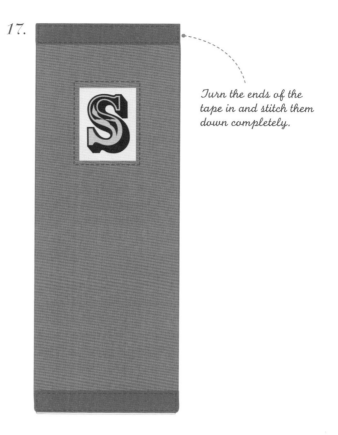

Turn the ends of the tape in and stitch them down completely.

18.

Even—or perhaps particularly—in the age of the smartphone, there's something special about a photograph album created to mark a memorable trip. This example was made in the colors of the Italian flag to commemorate a visit to Naples, but you can customize your version in whatever way is appropriate to your vacation.

PERSONALIZING YOUR PROJECT

• Anna is used here as a stencil, but would also lend itself particularly well to letters made from binding or tape, with its angled crossbars and sharp, folded corners.

ABOUT THE FONT

ANNA

Named for the daughter of its designer, Daniel Pelavin, Anna was first used on his wedding invitation. Designed in 1991, this uppercase-only font has a somewhat 1920s appeal—it would seem at home on an Art Deco movie house canopy.

YOU WILL NEED

Small photograph album; ours measured about 6 x 8 in. (15 x 20 cm)

Laminating machine and laminating pouches

Sheet of brown paper

White cotton fabric; for our album we required 30 x 5 in. (76 x 12.5 cm)

Two 12-in. (31-cm) squares of corrugated cardboard

Sheets of white paper

Red fabric paint

Synthetic dish-washing sponge

Fusible web; for our album we required 30 x 5 in. (76 x 12.5 cm)

Firm iron-on fusible interfacing; for our album we required 30 x 8 in. (76 x 20 cm)

Thin green cotton fabric; for our album we required 30 x 8 in. (76 x 20 cm)

Green sewing thread

Craft knife

Cloth tape measure

Metal ruler

Straight pins

Much of the character of Anna comes from its low and sharp-edge crossbars.

Making the album cover

1 Assemble the word and date you want on your album and print them out to scale. The country or city name is about 1¾ inches (4.5 cm) high, and the date is about 1¼ inches (3 cm). Laminate the name and date using the laminating machine and a pouch.

2 Using the craft knife and a metal ruler, cut out the letters and numbers. Cut out the holes in any characters or numbers, such as "0," "A," or "P," but keep them to one side; you can pin them in position on the stencil later.

3 Use the tape measure to measure the height and the thickness at the top and bottom of the photo album. Add ⅛ inch (3 mm) to this overall measurement.

4 To make the pattern for the album cover, cut a long strip of brown paper to the height worked out in step 3. Wrap it around the album to calculate the length; it should wrap right around the outside of the album and extend inside the front and back covers to just over half the album's width. Cut the brown paper strip to the right length.

2.

If you can choose a relatively short word, your album cover will have more impact.

3.

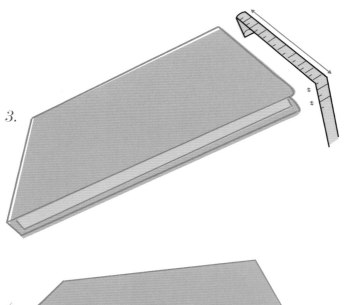

4.

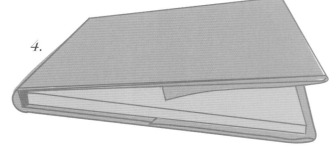

5 Unfold the cover pattern. Cut the strip of white cotton into two lengths a little longer than required—one for the name and one for the date. The name strip should extend from at least the full width of the back flap to just beyond the right-hand edge of the front cover; the date strip should extend from at least two-thirds of the way across the front cover to the full width of the front flap.

6 Place the two squares of corrugated cardboard, one on top of the other, on your work surface and place some sheets of plain paper on top of them. Lay the right-hand end of the strip of white cotton for the place word (in this case, "Napoli") on top of this, then use pins to hold the word stencil to it, pinning through to the cardboard. Pin down any cutout centers of the letters, too, using two pins each to keep them from rotating.

7 Cut a small piece of foam from the dish-washing sponge, a little wider than the lines of the stencil. Pour a small quantity of the fabric paint onto a scrap of laminated paper and dab the sponge around in it until it is evenly covered. Dab it on a spare corner of paper to get rid of any excess, then gently dab it onto the stencil, building up the paint until the color is solid. Repeat with the date stencil on the second strip of cotton, positioning the date near the left-hand end of the strip of cotton.

8 Fix the fabric paint with a hot iron, following the manufacturer's instructions.

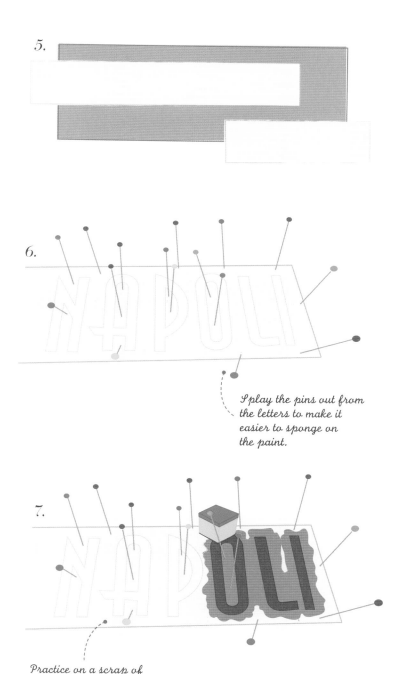

5.

6.

Splay the pins out from the letters to make it easier to sponge on the paint.

7.

Practice on a scrap of fabric to judge the right amount of pressure to put on the sponge.

9 Following the manufacturer's instructions, apply fusible web to the back of the cotton strips.

10 Using a craft knife and a metal ruler, trim the edges of the fabric strips so that they are parallel and evenly spaced around the lettering and the date. Cut a straight edge at the end of the word ("Napoli") and at the beginning of the date.

11 Press the iron-on interfacing onto the piece of colored cotton fabric. Lay the paper pattern on the wrong side of the fabric and draw around it, adding a ½-inch (12-mm) seam allowance on the two long sides. Cut out the fabric.

12 Fold the fabric around the album, making sure that the short sides are parallel with the edges and that the flaps are the same size. Place the lettered strips in position, aligning them with the album edges and making sure they're parallel with one another, too. When you are happy with their positions, mark their corners with a pencil.

13 Take the fabric off the album, peel off the backing paper from the fusible web, position the strips on the fabric and press in place.

9.

Make sure the edges of the strips are exactly parallel with the edges of the characters.

10.

NAPOLI

2014

12.

NAPOLI

2014

14 Fold the short ends of the fabric over by ½ inch (12 mm) and press flat. Thread the sewing machine with green thread and stitch the raw edges down.

15 Wrap the fabric around the album again, making sure that the flaps are the same size. On the outside of the cover, mark the points where the flaps end.

16 Take the fabric off. With right sides together, fold the flaps back to the marked points on the outside of the cover and pin in place. Machine stitch along the top and bottom edges of the flaps, ½ inch (12 mm) from the raw edges, reverse stitching at the start and finish to secure. Snip off the corners, close to the seam.

17 Turn the cover right side out, pushing out the corners with scissor points or the tip of a pencil. Press flat, then turn under the ½-inch (12-mm) seam allowances along the top and bottom edges and press them flat.

18 Right side up, topstitch a line along the top and bottom edges of the album cover, 1/16 inch (1–2 mm) from the edge, reverse stitching at the start and finish.

19 Put the cover on the album. Any puckers or wrinkles can be gently pressed out by using a warm iron through a clean dish towel.

14.

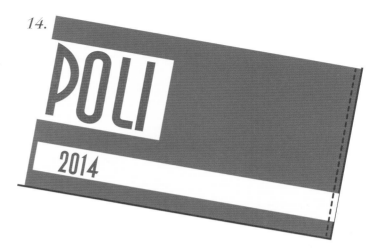

16.

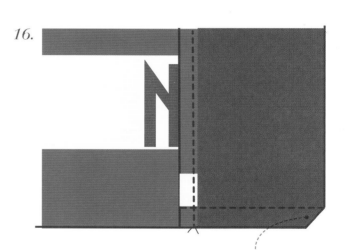

Trimming the corners will help to make sharp corners when the cover is turned the right way out.

18.

The zippy, upbeat look of this font is reminiscent of signwriting and is perfectly suited to the kitchen—if you argue with your chef partner, at least you can make sure that your apron agrees with you! The letters are elaborate, but you'll find the stencil relatively easy to cut, especially if you use a laminating machine to make it. If you live in a household with a lot of enthusiastic cooks, you could make a matching set of aprons with different-color stripes and an appropriate phrase for each one. Before you start, test the paints on the fabrics you intend to use to check that the paint doesn't bleed.

PERSONALIZING YOUR PROJECT

- With script fonts like this, plan out your word or phrase and experiment with different sizes to get the best balance for your project.
- Candy Script has a variety of different forms for each character in the alphabet, allowing you to create a range of looks with the same font.

ABOUT THE FONT

Created in 2007 by the Argentinian type designer Alejandro Paul, Candy Script was invented to celebrate the hand-painted signage seen all over South America.

YOU WILL NEED

Template on page 124

Plain calico apron

2 fl. oz. (50 ml) bright red fabric paint

1 fl. oz. (25 ml) navy blue fabric paint

Laminating machine and laminating pouch

Two 12-in. (31-cm) squares of corrugated cardboard

Few sheets of plain paper

Synthetic dish-washing sponge

11-in. (28-cm) square of mid-weight white cotton fabric (for the lettered patch)

11-in. (28-cm) square of fusible web

White sewing thread

Craft knife

Sharp scissors

Cutting mat

Red pencil

1-in. (2.5-cm) paintbrush

1-yd. (1-m) metal ruler

Straight pins

Check the variety of letterforms available if you want to create your own message—you'll often find two or three variants.

Making the apron

1 Press your apron flat and lay it on a flat surface. Use the ruler to find the center point of the bib and draw a vertical center line all the way down the apron with the red pencil.

2 Mark two more lines 1 inch (2.5 cm) away from each side of the center line—these outer two lines mark the width of the centered red stripe (2 inches/5 cm). Continue to work outward from the center line, marking red stripes that are 2 inches (5 cm) wide and 1 inch (2.5 cm) apart.

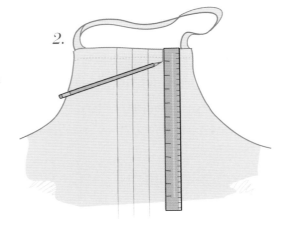

3 Shake the red fabric paint thoroughly before you open the container. Lay the apron on a flat surface protected with several layers of newspaper and paint the red stripes, following the pencil lines. Don't be too careful with the edges; the end effect is supposed to look hand-painted.

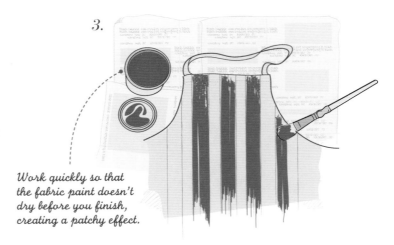

Work quickly so that the fabric paint doesn't dry before you finish, creating a patchy effect.

4 Fix the paint with a hot iron, following the manufacturer's instructions.

5 Photocopy or scan the template on page 124, enlarging it to scale, and print it out. Laminate the printout in the laminator. Use a craft knife on a cutting mat to cut the letters out to create a stencil. Cut out the centers of both "Es," but retain the pieces so that they can be pinned in place when you're using the stencil.

6 Lay out the two squares of corrugated cardboard, one on top of the other, then lay a couple of layers of plain paper on top, and finally the mid-weight cotton fabric square.

7 Pin the stencil onto the cotton, pushing the pins through the cotton and paper and into the cardboard to hold them in place. Place the pins as shown, pointing outward from the holes in the stencil (this will make it easier to sponge the paint in place). Pin the centers of the "Es" in place with two upright pins so that the centers won't rotate.

8 Cut a piece of foam from the dish-washing sponge, just a tiny bit wider than the lines of the letters.

9 Shake the navy blue fabric paint thoroughly, then open the container and pour a little onto a scrap piece of the laminated paper. Dab the sponge around in it until it is evenly covered, then dab it up and down on a paint-free piece of paper to remove any excess. Dab the sponge gently through the stencil, building up the color until the letter areas are solidly colored.

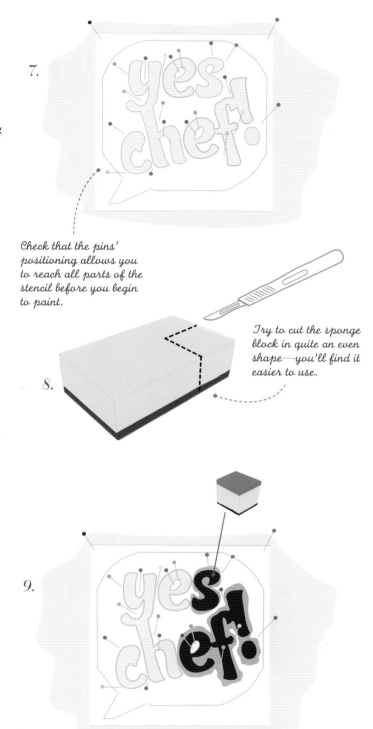

7.

Check that the pins' positioning allows you to reach all parts of the stencil before you begin to paint.

Try to cut the sponge block in quite an even shape—you'll find it easier to use.

8.

9.

10 Let the paint dry before removing the stencil from the fabric, then fix the fabric paint with a hot iron, following the manufacturer's instructions.

11 Print out a second copy of the template and cut around the speech bubble. Press the square of fusible web onto the back of the lettered patch. Place the template on top of the lettered patch and draw around the speech bubble using a pencil, then cut it out.

12 Make sure the apron is laying flat. Peel the paper backing off the fusible web and position the speech bubble on the front of the apron, then lay a dish towel over it and iron the patch on, following the manufacturer's instructions.

13 For a neat finish, thread the sewing machine with white thread and sew around the edge of the patch with a zigzag stitch.

11.

12.

Stitching the edge in a zigzag will make the patch sturdier as well as looking neat.

Plastic tablecloths are available in plenty of summery, upbeat patterns that combine well with some bold, simple font application to make your personal take on a waterproof picnic blanket. Keep it in the car trunk so that you can indulge alfresco when the sun's shining but the grass is still damp.

PERSONALIZING YOUR PROJECT

- The broad shapes of Stone Sans make it ideal if you're not confident about cutting narrow links on letters. It works well at most scales, and makes for simply stencil cutting.

ABOUT THE FONT

Stone Sans

Named for its designer, Sumner Stone, Stone Sans is part of a font family he created in 1987, when he was director of typography for Adobe. Solid but stylish, it cooperates well with other fonts, but this project showcases it working solo.

YOU WILL NEED

60 in. (1.5 m) patterned plastic tablecloth, 55 in. (140 cm) wide

39 in. (1 m) plain plastic tablecloth, 59 in. (150 cm) wide

60 in. (1.5 m) ripstop fabric, rubber-backed if possible, 59 in. (150 cm) wide

6½ yds. (6 m) cotton bias tape, 1 in. (2.5 cm) wide

Sewing thread to match the patterned tablecloth, ripstop fabric, and bias tape

Scissors

Fine marker or ball-point pen

Pencil

Tape measure

Masking tape

Straight pins

The forms of Stone Sans are often quirkier than they first appear—here, look at the joints on the "K," or the curl of the "P."

Making the blanket

1 Measure the width of the patterned tablecloth and cut the length to match, so that you have a square piece. If it is creased from storage, you can relax the folds and flatten the cloth with a hair dryer set to warm.

2 Print out your letters, with the tallest (in our case, the "p") enlarged so that it is 19 inches (48 cm) high. For some letters, you may need to use multiple sheets of paper that you combine after printing. Cut the letters out; in our case, we needed to record the distance between the stem of the "i" and its dot so that we could position them correctly later.

3 Lay the plain tablecloth flat, pin the paper patterns onto the material, draw around them, and cut out the letters.

4 Find the centerpoint of your patterned tablecloth, then work out the positioning for your letters, so that they appear in two even lines in the middle of the sheet. For each line, lay a tape measure along where the base of the letters (without the "tails") should sit, then adhere short pieces of masking tape on the tablecloth, using the tape measure as a guide, to mark the position for each letter.

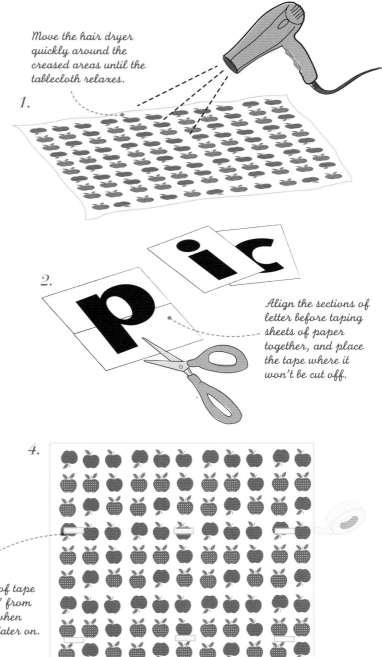

Move the hair dryer quickly around the creased areas until the tablecloth relaxes.

1.

2.

Align the sections of letter before taping sheets of paper together, and place the tape where it won't be cut off.

4.

Using short pieces of tape prevents the "tails" from getting in the way when removing the tape later on.

5 Starting with the center letter on the top row (in our case "i"), tape it in place on the patterned tablecloth using little pieces of masking tape.

6 Thread your sewing machine with thread to match the letter and, using a large zigzag stitch, sew around the letter. You'll find it easiest to do each character in two halves (so you're not trying to push the whole bulk of the patterned tablecloth through the machine at any point) and to roll it up on each side of each letter as you stitch, so you don't have to work with the whole size of the cloth. When you turn corners in the letters, leave the needle down in the fabric as you turn. Knot the threads at the back of the patterned tablecloth. Repeat steps 5 and 6 for the remaining letters.

7 Lay the ripstop fabric on the floor, wrong side up, and lay the patterned fabric on top of it, right side up. Use pieces of masking tape to adhere the patterned tablecloth down onto the ripstop.

8 Thread the sewing machine with thread to match the ripstop and stitch around the two layers, ¼ inch (6 mm) in from the edge of the patterned fabric. Trim the ripstop to the edge of the tablecloth.

9 Thread the sewing machine with thread to match the cotton bias tape. Begin attaching the tape, halfway along one side of the blanket, by first turning the end of the tape down at a 45-degree angle, as shown, before stitching.

5.

You can peel the tape pieces off the letters as you machine them.

7.

9.

10 Stop the stitches 1½ inches (4 cm) from the corner of the blanket. Fold the tape at a right angle, moving the tape away from the blanket and aligned to the bottom of the blanket, then fold it back on itself to run along the adjoining edge of the blanket. Now, fold the "triangle flap" at the corner down and continue stitching to the crease in the fold, then finish the stitches by making a few stitches back and forth.

11 Take the blanket out of the machine and start stitching again on the other side of the fold ½ inch (1 cm) from where you just finished stitching the tape folded underneath. Continue in this way until you return to the starting point. Snip off any excess tape just beyond where you stop stitching. Go back and forth for a few stitches to secure the end.

12 Fold the bias tape over to the back of the blanket, enclosing the edges of the blanket. Begin pinning down the bias tape along one edge, covering the stitches.

13 At the corner, after pinning the bias in place along one edge, fold over the adjoining edge, which should form a neat mitered corner. Pin in place, then continue until the bias is pinned down all around. Stitch it down neatly, sewing just inside the inner edge of the tape.

After one edge is pinned down, turn the tape at the corner over to make a mitred fold with straight edges.

10.

12.

13.

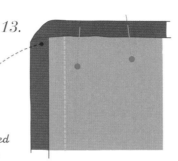 

{Leather & Canvas} Shopper

This solid shopper is made from a mixture of thin leather and heavyweight drill, with durable rope handles. Franklin Gothic has supplied the necessary bold letter for the appliqué, to make the best use of the red/green color contrast, and sans serif suits the clean shape well, but the simplicity of the design means that you could adapt pretty much any font or letter according to taste. If you're not used to topstitching on your machine, experiment on scraps of drill and leather before you put the bag together.

PERSONALIZING YOUR PROJECT

• Even, solid, and straightforward to cut out, this font is a good pick for projects using letters that need to be readable at a distance.

ABOUT THE FONT

FRANKLIN GOTHIC

Issued by American Type Founders in 1902, and designed by one of the early twentieth century's star typographers, Morris Fuller Benton, Franklin Gothic was an immediate hit and has been one of the most widely used sans serif fonts ever since.

Undramatic but distinctive, the Franklin Gothic family offers a whole range of compressed and condensed weights—so it's also a good choice if you want to fit a word into a tight space in a project.

YOU WILL NEED

15½-in. (40-cm) length of heavy cotton drill in a natural color, 58 in. (147 cm) wide

20-in. (51-cm) square of green leather

Piece of thin red leather or leatherette (check your letter template for size before buying)

Sewing thread in red

Topstitch thread in green and cream

Four silver eyelets with washers, $\frac{7}{16}$ in. (11 mm) in diameter

2 yds. (2 m) twisted rope cord, $\frac{5}{16}$ in. (8 mm) in diameter

Leather sewing machine needle

Denim sewing machine needle

Eyelet maker

Sharp scissors

Fabric marking pen

Pencil

High-tack craft glue

Tape measure

Masking tape

Straight pins

Making the shopper

1 Cut out two rectangles from the cotton drill, each measuring 19 x 10½ inches (49 x 27 cm). Cut out one rectangle from the green leather, measuring 19 x 17 inches (49 x 43 cm).

2 Machine stitch around the edges of the drill rectangles, using zigzag stitch to stop them from fraying.

3 Place a cotton drill rectangle on each longer 19-inch (49-cm) side of the leather. Run a fine line of high-tack craft glue along the sides of the two cotton drill rectangles abutting the leather and adhere the leather down onto the cotton drill, overlapping it by about ½ inch (12 mm). Let dry.

4 Thread the sewing machine with green topstitch thread and, using a leather needle, run a large zigzag stitch along each glued seam of the leather.

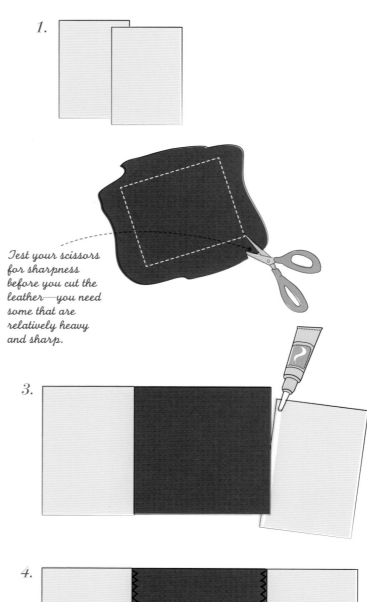

Test your scissors for sharpness before you cut the leather—you need some that are relatively heavy and sharp.

5 Print out your letter, enlarged to 10 inches (25.5 cm) tall, and cut it out.

6 Fold the drill/leather rectangle in half lengthwise, wrong sides together, and use a tape measure and a fabric marking pen to find and mark the center point of the rectangle's width. Unfold the rectangle.

7 Place your paper letter template at the center point and position it so that the bottom of the template falls about 4 inches (10 cm) below the edge of the leather. When you've got your template straight, mark the corners of the template onto the drill and leather, using the fabric marking pen.

8 Use the paper pattern to draw around and cut out your letter from the thin red leather. Adhere it in place on the side of the bag, using high-tack craft glue and using the guide points you drew in the previous step. Let dry.

7.

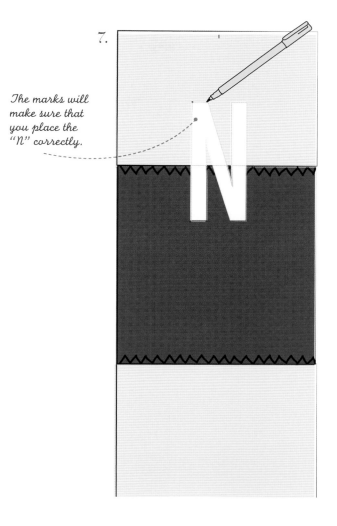

The marks will make sure that you place the "N" correctly.

8.

9 Using the leather needle on the sewing machine and red thread, zigzag stitch around the letter.

10 Fold the rectangle in half again, this time right sides together, and machine stitch the side seams, using a running stitch and stitching ½ inch (12 mm) in from the edges. Reverse stitch for about 1 inch (2.5 cm) at the beginning and end of each seam to strengthen it.

11 To make the corners and give the bag a flat bottom, fold the bag as shown in the diagram so that the side seams are aligned in the center and the corners of the leather stick out in a triangle at the bottom.

12 Open out the leather seam of one of the corners and tape it down, open, with two strips of masking tape. Using a ruler and a fabric marking pen, mark a line at 90 degrees to the seam and 5 inches (12.5 cm) long from edge to edge.

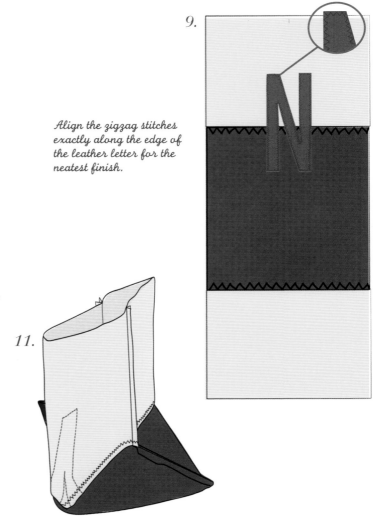

9.

Align the zigzag stitches exactly along the edge of the leather letter for the neatest finish.

11.

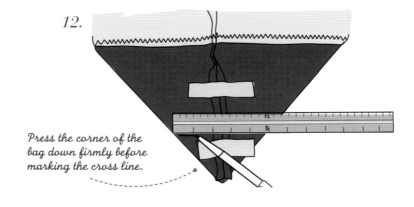

12.

Press the corner of the bag down firmly before marking the cross line.

13 Thread your machine with green thread and, using a leather needle, stitch along the drawn line, reverse stitching for about 1 inch (2.5 cm) at the beginning and end of the seam to strengthen it. Cut off the corner ⅜ inch (1 cm) below the stitching. Repeat on the other corner of the bag.

14 Mark a pencil line 2 inches (5 cm) down from the raw edge of the drill on the wrong side, then fold the raw edge down to meet the line and press the crease with a hot iron. Turn the edge down again, so that you have a double fold, and press again.

15 Thread your machine with cream thread and, using a denim needle, stitch along the turned-under edge ¼ inch (6 mm) in from the fold.

16 Turn the bag right side out and mark the center top of each side with a pin. Using a fabric marking pen, make a mark 4 inches (10 cm) away from each side of the center mark. Use the eyelet maker to set the eyelets in place at each marked point, ⅜ inch (1 cm) down from the top edge of the bag.

17 Cut the rope cord in half and make the handles, tying tight knots on the inside of the bag to hold them secure.

13.

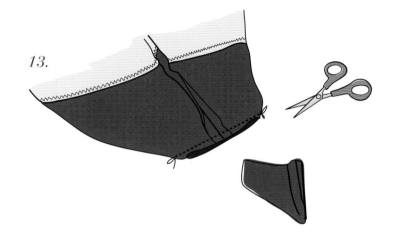

14.

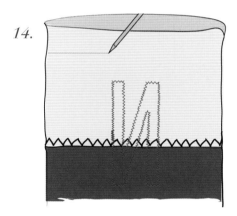

16.

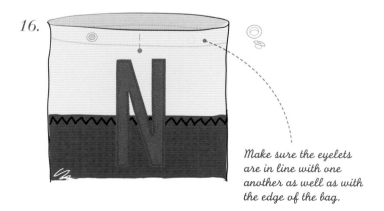

Make sure the eyelets are in line with one another as well as with the edge of the bag.

The vivid yellow of the linen in this project is a wonderful background for setting off the gray herringbone of the scripted message. The script is made from bias tape, appliquéd onto the linen; cutting the tape on the bias makes it stretchy, which makes it easier to pull the pieces into shape to match the flowing curves of the type. This project is probably a little more challenging than some others in the book, so do set aside a few evenings to make it. After making your own bias tape in two different widths, you need to follow the diagram to apply short pieces in a certain order—but it's satisfying to see the curves begin to echo the font exactly.

PERSONALIZING YOUR PROJECT

- If you choose your own phrase, you will find that the letters are thicker than your bias tape, so just use the tape around the outside edge of each letter.

ABOUT THE FONT

Santa Fe

Designed in the 1980s by the British designer David Quay, Santa Fe's curling shapes, elaborately rounded characters, and forward slant all give it an appealing go-faster feel.

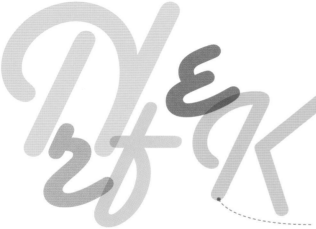

YOU WILL NEED

Template on pages 124–25

1-in. (2.5-cm) and ½-in. (12-mm) bias tape makers

2-yd. (2-m) length of bright yellow linen, 58 in. (147 cm) wide

1 yd. (1 m) thin, tight-woven herringbone fabric, 58 in. (147 cm) wide, in shades of brown, for the lettering; if you use another fabric, pick a thin but tight weave, such as a lightweight suiting material

Brown sewing thread to match font fabric

Embroidery needle

Embroidery hoop, 10 in. (25.5 cm) in diameter

1-yd. (1-m) metal ruler

Craft knife

Sharp scissors

Cutting mat

Fabric marking pen

Tape measure

Masking tape

Straight pins

The fluid character forms of Santa Fe are more legible in script than as individual letters.

Making the table runner

1 Photocopy or scan the template on pages 124–25, enlarging it to scale. You will need to print it out onto several sheets of paper, so tape them together to make a single pattern.

2 Cut out the type neatly with a craft knife to make a stencil.

3 Follow the manufacturer's instructions to use the bias tape maker to make two lengths of bias tape from the brown herringbone fabric cut on the bias. You will need 5 yards (4.5 m) of 1-inch (2.5-cm)-wide tape and 6 yards (5.5 m) of ½-inch (12-mm)-wide tape. You will be using it in short pieces, so there is no need to join the strips together after you cut them. The ½-inch (12-mm) tape will be used for the lettering; the 1-inch (2.5-cm) tape, for the binding around the edge of the runner.

4 Cut a 19½-inch (50-cm) strip from the linen. Press the remaining linen so that it is crease free and secure it to your work surface with masking tape. Find and mark the midpoint of the fabric's length. Lay the paper stencil over the fabric, matching the midpoints (the midpoint of the stencil should be the top of the vertical of the first "p" in "appétit").

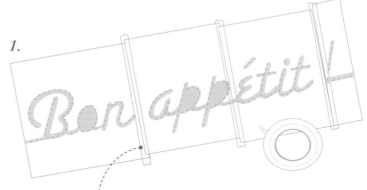

1.

Tape the paper front and back to strengthen the joints.

3.

Simply pull the fabric strips through the tape maker—it does the work for you.

You will need to add strip 3 before you lay out the curved section of strip 1.

5 Pin the stencil to the linen and draw around it using the fabric marking pen. Use a ruler to extend the lines that run from the base of the initial "B" and the exclamation mark. Remove the tape from the linen so that you can start to stitch the lettering.

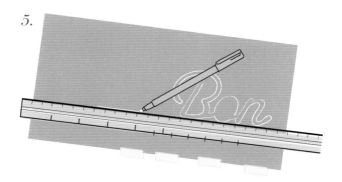

6 The letters are pieced together from the short lengths of bias tape cut in step 3. The order in which the tape is applied is shown in the diagram on the previous page; look carefully at the diagram as you work, because it makes the order of stitching clear by showing which pieces of tape overlay others. Start with the "B," taking one of the longer pieces of the ½-inch (12-mm) tape (it needs to be long enough to complete the letter). Pin the tape in from the left-hand side of the linen to just before the vertical of the "B."

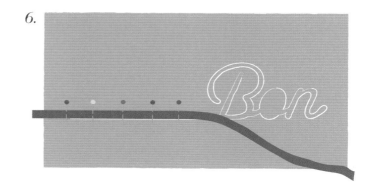

7 Using small slip stitches, sew the bottom edge of the tape down to the point at which the vertical of the "B" starts, then cut a piece of tape to make the vertical, leaving enough extra tape at the end to fold it down. Pin the vertical in position and place the linen in an embroidery hoop, pulling tight, to stitch it.

8 Stitch the vertical, using small slip stitches, then continue with a short length to join the "B" and the "o"; this needs to be sewn before you complete the "B," as shown on the diagram. Stitch the outside edges before the inside edges.

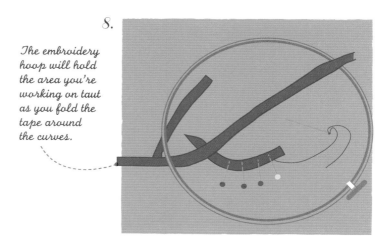

The embroidery hoop will hold the area you're working on taut as you fold the tape around the curves.

9 When you have sewn the linking piece (marked 3 on the diagram), complete the curves of the "B". You will need to make a fold in the tape between the two curves.

10 Remove the linen from the embroidery hoop and press it, then put the hoop back, moving it to the right on the linen so that you can complete working on the "o."

11 Take a length of tape long enough for the whole of the "o," the link between the "o" and the "n," and the upright stroke of the "n." Pin the tape in place over the word outline and stitch around the outer edge of the "o," making a tuck where shown on the stitching diagram.

12 Sew the inside edge of the "o" and stitch down the tuck. Stitch up the left side of the tape that makes the upright of the "n." Tuck in the end of the upright and stitch down.

13 Move the embroidery hoop so that it contains the whole of the letter "n." Cut a piece of tape to make the rest of the "n," cut the end at an angle, and tuck it into the open right-hand side of the upright. Stitch down the right-hand side of the upright.

9.

11.

Pin every character completely, taking in the extra fabric on the curves, before you start to stitch.

13.

14 Pin and stitch the remainder of the "n" along the outside edge, making a tuck at the bottom of the curve, as shown on the stitching diagram. Turn in the raw end and stitch, then sew the inside edge of the "n."

15 Continue following the stitching diagram in the same way to complete "appétit!," moving the embroidery hoop to the right as necessary and pressing the linen between characters. Stitch the tape to run off the linen from the period of the exclamation mark, stitching the end down at the edge of the linen.

16 Tape the linen back to your work surface. The runner will measure 70 by 12½ inches (178 by 32 cm) long. Measuring from the center mark, trim the four sides ready to bind around the edges.

17 Open out one end of the 1-inch (2.5-cm) tape, laying it face down on the right side of the runner, starting halfway up one of the short edges. Turn the end of the tape over at a 45-degree angle (see step 9, page 84) before stitching. Pin the binding in place up to the corner of the runner.

18 "Miter" the corners of the runner as you pin, folding the bias tape away from the fabric at right angles to make an L-shape when you reach a corner, and then folding it back down on itself along the adjoining edge and pinning it in place.

14.

16.

Press the runner lightly before trimming the edges to straight lines at each end.

18.

19 When you have pinned the tape all around the runner, thread the sewing machine with matching thread and stitch the tape in place, sewing along the first fold line of the tape. See steps 10 and 11 on page 85 for instructions on stitching at the corner.

20 Press the tape from the front of the runner, using a steam iron. At the corners, press 45-degree folds with the tape from the long sides of the runner on top of the fold.

21 Turn the runner over and fold the tape over to the back of the runner, pressing the short ends so that the edge of the tape aligns with the line of stitching.

22 Press the tape on the long sides of the runner on the back, making folds in the corners. Stitch the corners down by hand, then sew along the length of the tape using small slip-stitches.

20.

21.

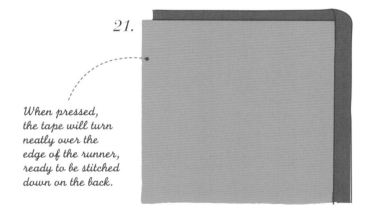

When pressed, the tape will turn neatly over the edge of the runner, ready to be stitched down on the back.

22.

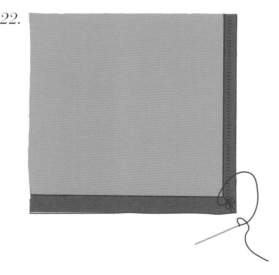

The best-ever, handmade way to mark a big occasion or send a special message, you only need to master a basic pennant structure to customize this banner of flags. Our "Happy New Year" materials allow for twelve letters, but you can size up or down to make any message you want. We've used a clean-cut inline font; the internal line within each letter, along with a contrasting color of surround, will make sure it reads easily at a distance.

PERSONALIZING YOUR PROJECT

- Inline letters look clean and crisp, but for obvious reasons, it's nearly impossible to reproduce the whole characters as stencils. For fabric, they work best with appliquéd bias tape.

ABOUT THE FONT

CYCLONE

Designed by Hoefler & Frere-Jones, based in New York, Cyclone is a slightly elongated inline font. There are alternatives for six characters to enable you to change the mood visually.

MnOyX

Try black and white as well as colorful mixes—monochromatic in contrasting materials will look good.

YOU WILL NEED

Templates on page 127

1 yd. (1 m) fusible web

8-in. (20-cm) square each of bright pink, turquoise, and yellow felt

Two 8-in. (20-cm) squares of orange felt

24-in. (61-cm) piece of blue silk, 115 cm (45 in.) wide

24-in. (61-cm) piece of green silk, 115 cm (45 in.) wide

Sewing thread in pink, blue, green, turquoise, yellow, and orange

6½ yds. (6 m) gimp braid, ¼ in. (6 mm) wide

6½ yds. (6 m) bias tape, 1 in. (2.5 cm) wide

Craft knife and cutting mat

Sharp scissors

Hole punch

Fabric marking pen

High-tack craft glue

Metal ruler

Straight pins

Making the banner of flags

1 Make a quick sketch of your words so that you can plan the letter colors. We alternated pink, turquoise, yellow, and orange felt, but you could use fewer colors or even choose just one if you prefer a simpler effect.

2 Cut out a square of fusible web for each of the felt squares, trimming it to fit the squares exactly, and press with a warm iron to fuse a fusible web square to each of the felt squares.

3 Print out the letters, enlarged to 6¼ inches (16 cm) high, and cut them out neatly to make templates.

4 Reverse your letter templates, lay them on the wrong side of the felt squares, and draw around them with a fabric marking pen. (Check your plan to make sure that you're cutting each letter from the right color of felt.)

5 Cut the letters out of the felt. For the neatest finish, cut the straight lines with a metal ruler and a craft knife and the curves with a small, sharp pair of scissors.

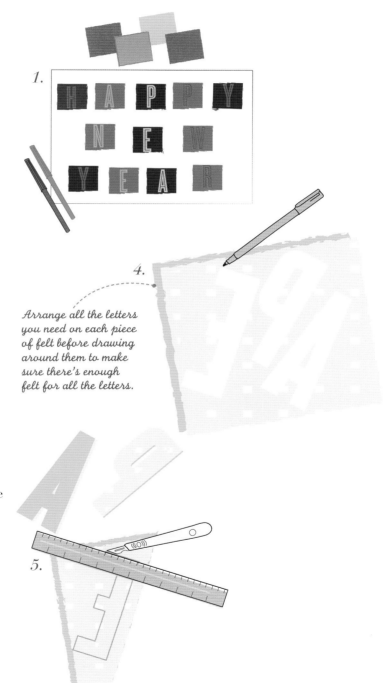

1.

4.

Arrange all the letters you need on each piece of felt before drawing around them to make sure there's enough felt for all the letters.

5.

6 Photocopy or scan the templates on page 127, enlarging them to scale, then print and cut them out. Cut 12 flag shapes from the blue silk and 10 from the green using the smaller template, adding a 1-inch (2.5-cm) seam allowance around each shape. Cut 2 flag shapes from the green silk using the wider template for the "W" (it needs more room than the other letters), adding a 1-inch (2.5-cm) seam allowance around each shape.

7 Fold the template along the vertical fold line, place it on the front of a flag shape, and use the fabric marking pen to mark a vertical line down the flag, then unfold. Now, fold the template down at the horizontal fold line and mark this line on the flag. Mark six of the blue and six of the green flag shapes in this way.

8 Peel the backing paper off the felt letters and center them on the prepared flag shapes along the vertical line and below the horizontal line, matching the colors to the plan and using the marking lines as placement guides.

9 Press the letters onto the flag pieces with a warm iron, using a clean dish towel between the iron and the fabric.

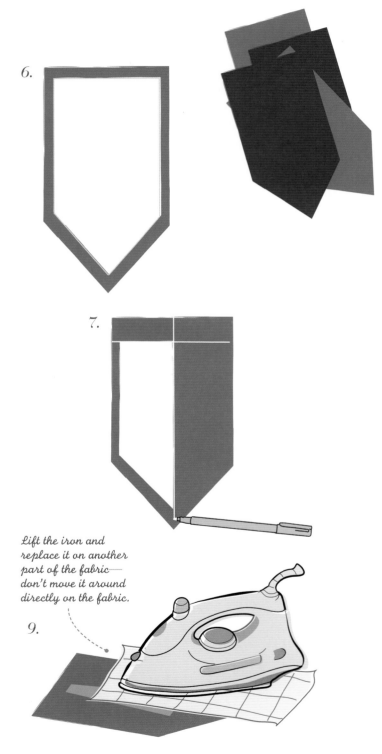

6.

7.

Lift the iron and replace it on another part of the fabric— don't move it around directly on the fabric.

9.

10 When all the letters are in place, thread the sewing machine with pink thread and stitch around the pink letters with a small zigzag stitch. Rethread the machine with thread in each of the other felt colors in turn and stitch around all the letters.

11 Use the fabric marking pen to mark the position for placing the braid inside each felt letter. Use a hole punch—or a pencil will do—to make holes in the letter template along the top and base of each section of the letter and at cross sections, stopping the lines about ½ inch (12 mm) short of the ends, depending on the the size of the template.

12 Use a craft knife to cut small slits the width of the braid through both the felt and silk backing at all the pairs of dots on each letter.

13 Now, apply the braid to the center line of the letters. Starting with the letter "H," cut a length of braid 2 inches (5 cm) longer than the horizontal line and use the points of a pair of scissors to push it through the slits to the back.

14 Insert two pins into the braid where it meets the slits, then pull the braid back up a little, but not out of the slits. Glue the back of the braid between the two pins. Pull the ends from the back of the flag so the braid lies flat and let dry.

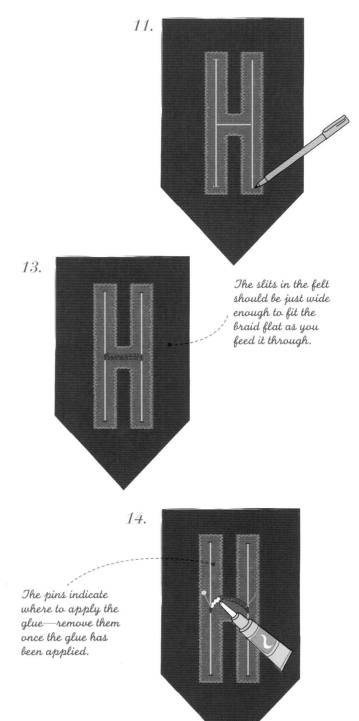

11.

13.

The slits in the felt should be just wide enough to fit the braid flat as you feed it through.

14.

The pins indicate where to apply the glue—remove them once the glue has been applied.

15 To make the sides of the "H," cut two lengths of braid, each 2 inches (5 cm) longer than the length of the sides. As before, mark the area to be glued with pins, glue the back of each length of braid, and secure in place. Let dry.

16 Glue down all the ends on the back. Repeat steps 13 to 16 for each flag.

17 Place the paper pattern on the back of each lettered flag piece, using the folds to line it up centered with the letter, then draw around it with the fabric marking pen.

18 Line up each lettered flag piece with a plain flag the same color, right sides together. Sew around the side and bottom edges of the drawn template outline, leaving the top open. Trim the seam allowances to ½ inch (1 cm). Turn the flags the right way around and press.

19 Use the ruler and marking pen to draw a line 1 inch (2.5 cm) above the lettering on each of the flags.

20 Cut the bias tape into two equal lengths. Mark the center point of one piece with a pin, open the tape out, and pin the first "P" of "HAPPY" in place, along the line drawn on the top edge of the letter. Pin on the rest of the letters, leaving a 1-inch (2.5-cm) gap between each flag.

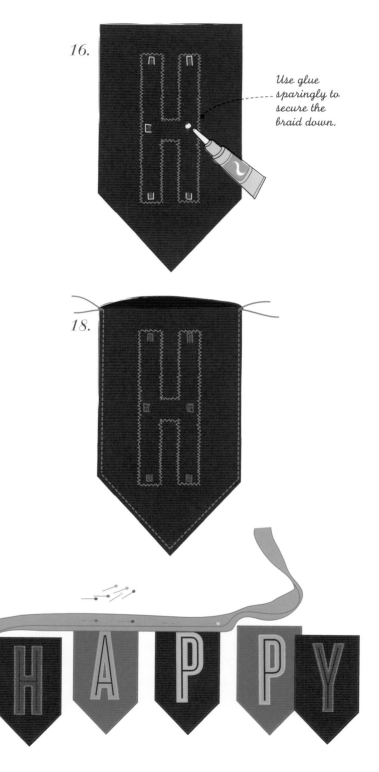

16.

Use glue sparingly to secure the braid down.

18.

20.

21 Mark the center point of the second piece of tape and pin the left-hand corner of the "Y" of "YEAR" under it. Add the letters in the same way as before, leaving 1-inch (2.5-cm) gaps between them, except between the "W" and the "Y," which should have a 3-inch (7.5-cm) gap to mark the space between the words.

22 Machine stitch the tape onto the flags. Trim off the top of each flag just below the edge of the tape.

23 Fold the other side of the tape over the top edge of the flags and press it so that the edge lines up with the existing line of stitching.

24 Stitch along the full length of the tape, taking in the flags as you work (make sure you place the banner in the machine the right way up). Fold in the raw ends of the tape and stitch closed.

A large-scale monogram transforms an everyday striped duvet or comforter cover. This one is confected with a mixture of fabric paint and custom-made bias tape and, with its mix of navy and white on a striped cover, it has a neat, nautical effect. It's worth adding to your craft kit a bias tape maker; they're inexpensive and you'll find that homemade bias tape is invaluable in dozens of craft applications. However, if you're time is short or you want to keep it simple, you can buy commercial white bias tape.

PERSONALIZING YOUR PROJECT

- Real grosgrain two-color ribbon with a single centered stripe can be used to re-create inline letters—it's simpler than a combined stencil-and-appliqué approach, although you may not be able to imitate the font precisely.

ABOUT THE FONT

RIBBON

The Philadelphia designer Dan Kneiding created Ribbon for the Lost Type Co-op. The V-cut ends give this uppercase-only font a distinctive look.

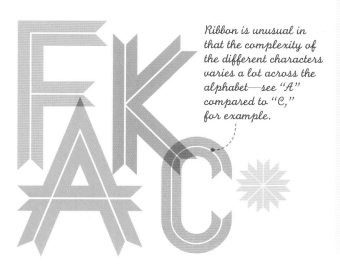

Ribbon is unusual in that the complexity of the different characters varies a lot across the alphabet—see "A" compared to "C," for example.

YOU WILL NEED

Sheets of letter-size paper to print and copy on; you'll need enough for 3 letters, each 15 in. (38 cm) high

Laminating machine and laminating pouch

Cotton or polycotton duvet or comforter cover; the blue stripe on the example we used contrasts well with the strong navy monogram, but you could use a plain cover if you prefer and alter the color of the fabric paint to match or contrast

Sheet of brown paper

23 x 33 in. (58 x 84 cm) sheet of cardboard

Navy fabric paint

30 in. (76 cm) white cotton or polycotton sheeting fabric, 7 ft. 6 in. (229 cm) wide, or store-bought white bias tape, ¼ in. (6 mm) wide

¼-in. (6-mm) bias tape maker

White sewing thread

Embroidery needle

Embroidery hoop, 10 in. (25 cm) in diameter

Dark and light chalk pencils plus normal pencil

Wide and narrow paintbrushes

Masking tape

Clear adhesive tape

Metal ruler

Cloth tape measure

Straight pins

Making the duvet cover

1 Print out your letters, enlarged to 15 inches (38 cm) tall. Place them in the top of the laminator pouch and laminate in the machine. Cut out and tape the pieces together.

2 Iron the duvet cover and spread it out on a flat surface.

3 Using the metal ruler and a chalk pencil, draw a line across the duvet cover 21 inches (54 cm) down from the top edge. Use the tape measure and ruler to find the center point of this line and mark it with a chalk pencil.

4 Mark and draw a second line 3 inches (7.5 cm) down from the first, 24 inches (61 cm) from the top edge.

5 Put loops of masking tape on the back of each letter template, so that they can be secured to the duvet cover.

6 Position the template for the middle letter of your monogram at the center point established across the width of the duvet cover, with its top edge aligning with the 21-inch (54-cm) line.

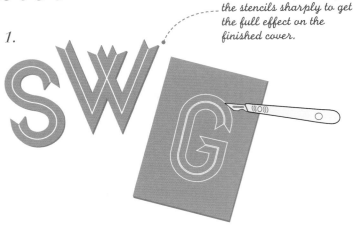

1.

Cut the ribbon points of the stencils sharply to get the full effect on the finished cover.

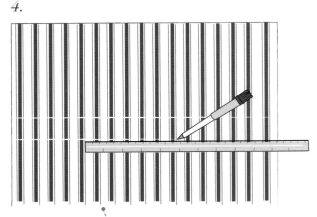

4.

Before you start, check that you have enough workspace to move around the duvet once it's laid flat.

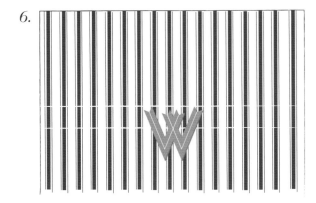

6.

7 Line up the other letter templates on each side of the centered letter, aligning the letter tops with the lower 24-inch (61-cm) line on the cover.

8 Draw around the templates with a sharp normal pencil, then remove them from the cover.

9 Tape the brown paper over the sheet of cardboard, securing it down at the corners.

10 Slip the cardboard inside the duvet cover, so that it's behind all three letters of the monogram; it will stop the fabric paint from bleeding through to the second layer of the cover. Once it's in position, don't move it until the letters are all painted and dry.

11 Use a fine paintbrush and fabric paint to paint the outlines of the three letters, then a wider brush to fill them in. Let the paint completely dry.

12 Fix the fabric paint with an iron, following the manufacturer's instructions. Wash the duvet cover.

8.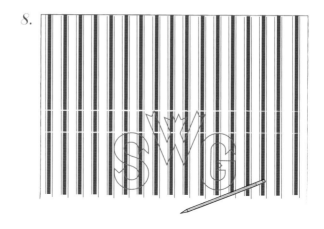

11.

Use the fabric paint sparingly and be careful not to overload the brush.

13 Use the tape measure to measure the centered ribbon stripe in each of the monogram's letters. From the white cotton sheeting, cut strips ⁹⁄₁₆ inch (14 mm) wide on the bias and use the tape maker to convert them into bias tape (you can use store-bought bias tape if you prefer).

14 Cut each of the letter templates into pieces along one side of the stripe/gap in the ribbon font.

15 Iron the washed duvet cover. Now, draw the center line for each letter, using the light chalk pencil, by laying pieces of the templates on top of the corresponding painted letter on the duvet cover. For some letters such as "S" and "G," you will just need to use one of the two halves of each template. For more complex letters, such as "W," which divide into more than two pieces, you will need to use some additional pieces.

16 If necessary, unpick a small gap in the middle of the top seam of the duvet cover (this is to enable you to get your hand in to stitch on the bias tape).

17 Fit the embroidery hoop around the top of the left-hand letter. Pin the bias tape along the chalked center line on the letter.

13.

15.

Hold the stencil down carefully as you draw the chalk guide lines.

17.

18 Thread an embroidery needle with white thread and slip-stitch the tape down onto the letter, stitching the first side of the tape over the chalk line. Fold under the end of the tape at the top end of the letter and stitch down the other side of the tape.

19 Remove the hoop and repeat step 18 around the lower half of the letter. (For larger characters, such as "W," you may need to reposition the hoop several times.)

20 Repeat steps 18 and 19 for the other two letters of the monogram.

21 Lay a clean dish towel over the letters and press them with a warm iron.

22 Slip-stitch the gap in the top seam of the duvet cover closed if necessary, or turn it inside out and stitch the gap closed with machine stitches.

18.

A small slip stitch is best for sewing the tape in place.

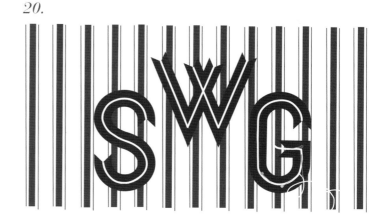

20.

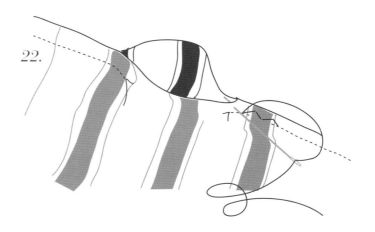

22.

Whether or not you're a cyclist, the classic messenger bag with its cross-body strap is invaluable for toting all your stuff. This version has everything you'd want: made from thin black leather, with reflective straps and your choice of letter. The initial letter appliqué is both glued and stitched, so it will stand up to the toughest treatment.

PERSONALIZING YOUR PROJECT

- We've created a shadow for the letter in this project, but the font looks just as strong without it.
- One of the rare faces with no straight lines, Hobo works well anywhere you want a flowing, organic shape to your type.

ABOUT THE FONT

Hobo

Created in 1910 by the American designer Morris Fuller Benton, Hobo is unusual in that all the characters rest on the same line, with no descenders.

Without descenders, this font is a good pick for any project that calls for characters to share a baseline.

YOU WILL NEED

Templates on pages 126–27

Large sheet of brown paper

Piece of thin black leather, at least 48 x 20 in. (121 x 51 cm)

12-in (31-cm.) square piece of yellow leatherette

8 x 10-in. (20 x 25.5-cm) piece of white leatherette

5-in. (13-cm) square of black leatherette

5-in. (13-cm) square of gray leatherette

80-in. (2-m) length of black nylon webbing, 1 in. (2.5 cm) wide

Two black plastic loops to fit webbing

11-in. (28-cm) length of hook-and-loop tape, 1 in. (2.5 cm) wide

45 in. (115 cm) reflective plastic tape, 1 in. (2.5 cm) wide

Black plastic buckle to fit webbing

Sewing thread in black, white, gray, and yellow

Sewing needle

Leather sewing machine needle

Thimble

Sharp scissors

Heavy-duty pair of scissors (to cut leather)

Ball-point pen

Pencil

High-tack craft glue

Latex-base contact adhesive

Small spatula or glue spreader

Masking tape

1-yd. (1-m) metal ruler

Straight pins

Making the messenger bag

1 Photocopy or scan the templates for the pieces of the bag on pages 126–27, enlarging them to scale, then print and cut them out. (You may need several sheets of paper for this; if so, overlap the pieces and tape them together.) Draw around the template pieces on brown paper to make the pattern and cut them out.

2 Copy or scan the templates for the bubbles on page 126, enlarging them to scale, then print and cut them out.

3 Enlarge the letter and period you want to use so that they fit easily within the height and width of the largest bubble. Print out the letter and period and cut them out. Lay the letter on the paper pattern for the bubble, and draw around it, then shift it slightly to the right and draw around it again. Repeat with the period shape; draw around it once, then move it slightly to the right and draw around it again.

4 Cut the overlapped letter and period shapes out of the bubble template.

5 Print out the letter and period two more times and cut them out.

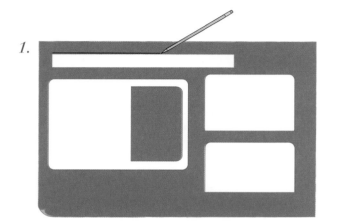

1.

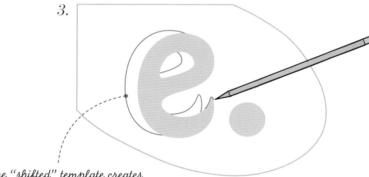

3.

The "shifted" template creates the shadow for the character on the finished bag.

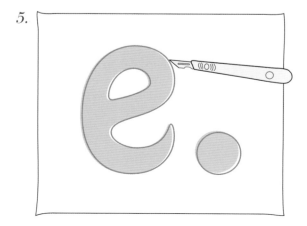

5.

6 Using the brown paper pattern for the bag and a ball-point pen, draw around the back-and-front-flap piece, the front piece, the underflap piece, and the side piece on the black leather and cut them out. Cut a second front piece out of the yellow leatherette.

7 Cut the three bubble shapes out of white leatherette (don't cut out the letter or the period). Cut one letter and period pair out of black leatherette, and cut a second out of gray leatherette.

8 Lay the bubble stencil over the largest white leatherette bubble and use a pencil to draw around the outline of the letter, the period, and their overlapping shadows.

9 Using the high-tack craft glue, adhere the gray leatherette letter and period to the right-hand outline of the pencil shape on the white leatherette.

10 Glue the black leatherette letter and period onto the left-hand outline of the pencil shape on the white leatherette, so that it overlaps with the gray shape (which forms its "shadow"), using high-tack craft glue. Let dry.

6.

9.

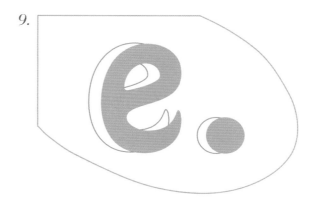

10.

Arrange the black letter over the gray one carefully, so the shadow around it appears evenly around the letter.

11 Spread the high-tack craft glue on the back of all three leatherette bubbles and glue them in place on the yellow leatherette flap piece. Let dry.

12 When the glue is dry, stab stitch around the edges of the gray and black letters, the period, and around the edges of all three bubbles, using matching threads, a sturdy needle and thimble.

13 Lay the yellow front piece on a flat surface. Take the back-and-front-flap piece of black leather and spread a thin line of high-tack craft glue around the inside edge of half the window. Carefully position the glued edge over the yellow front piece so that it is aligned within the window and glue it down. Now repeat for the second half of the window.

14 Using black thread and a leather needle in your sewing machine, sew around the frame on the flap, just inside the edge of the leather, reverse stitching at the start and finish of the seam to secure it. Trim off the excess yellow leatherette on the back of the flap.

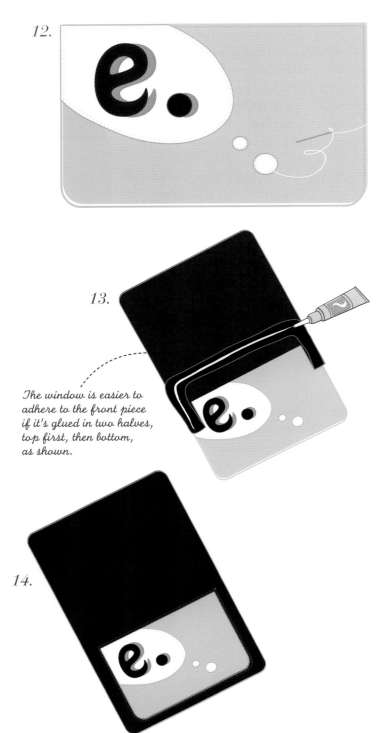

12.

13.

The window is easier to adhere to the front piece if it's glued in two halves, top first, then bottom, as shown.

14.

15 Cut two lengths of webbing, each 6 inches (15 cm) long. Thread 2 inches (5 cm) of each length through a plastic loop and pin that end 2 inches (5 cm) below the other end of the webbing. Stitch a line across the webbing near the loop, reverse stitching at the start and finish to secure.

16 Turn in the raw edges of the webbing and pin them in place.

17 Take the piece of leather that will form the sides of the bag and stitch the webbing loops in place 1 inch (2.5 cm) from each end, centered on the width. Place the raw edges against the leather, neat side out, and box stitch around the edges of the webbing pieces, as shown, for extra strength.

18 Pull the strip of hook-and-loop tape apart, and machine stitch the loop side onto the front of the black leather underflap of the bag, 1 inch (2.5 cm) from the curved edge and centered on the width. Sew the hook side of the tape onto the front of the black leather front piece, 2½ inches (6 cm) from the curved bottom edge and centered on the width.

15.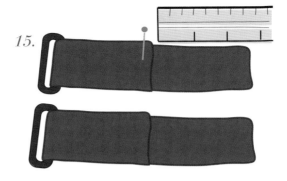

17.

18.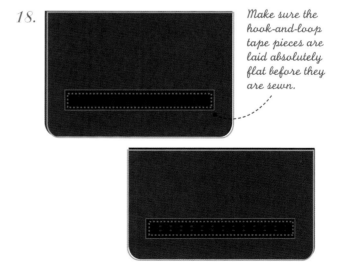

Make sure the hook-and-loop tape pieces are laid absolutely flat before they are sewn.

19 Using the contact adhesive and spatula, spread a thin line of adhesive along the edges on the wrong side of the window end of the back-and-front-flap piece and the black underflap piece. Let both pieces to dry for a few minutes, then align them carefully, wrong sides together, and press firmly together to adhere securely.

20 Machine stitch around the outside edge of the window in the front flap, 1/16 inch (2 mm) in from the edge.

21 Fold the strip for the sides of the bag in half and mark the center point on both edges on the back of the strip, using a ball-point pen. Fold the bag's front piece in half, right sides together, and mark the center point of the bottom edge. Repeat on the back-and-front-flap piece, on the other end from the window.

22 Using the contact adhesive and spatula, spread a thin line of adhesive around the side and bottom edges of the front of the bag on the reverse side, and another line all along one side of the strip for the sides. Let the glue dry for a minute, then align the side piece all along the edges of the front, matching the center marks together, and press firmly together to secure.

23 Machine stitch a line 3/16 inch (5 mm) along the side/front pieces where they have just been glued together.

19.

21.

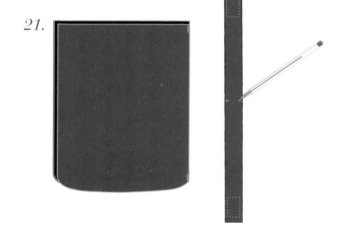

22.

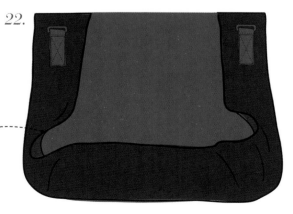

When the strip is firmly glued in place, it forms the gusset for the bag.

24 Repeat steps 22 and 23 to attach the back-and-front-flap piece of the bag to the side strip, first gluing and then stitching the seam.

25 Use high-tack craft glue to glue the upper edge of the underflap and the front of the bag together. Press firmly and let dry.

26 On a piece of webbing 55 inches (139 cm) long, stitch a 45-inch (115-cm) length of reflective tape to it, leaving a 6-inch (15-cm) length of webbing uncovered at one end, and using yellow thread.

27 Thread the plastic buckle onto the 6-inch (15-cm) length of webbing free at one end of the strap. Fold the raw end in and pin it down to the strap 1 inch (2.5 cm) from the end of the reflective tape, then machine stitch across the strap to secure.

28 Thread the loose (buckle-free) end of the strap through one of the plastic loops on the bag, with the reflective tape facing inwards and then back up through the buckle and through the loop on the other side of the bag. Fold in the raw edge of the webbing and stitch it down.

25.

26.

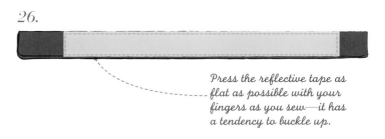

Press the reflective tape as flat as possible with your fingers as you sew—it has a tendency to buckle up.

27.

Templates

{BABY} BLOCKS
Shown actual size.

{ONE-LETTER} DOORSTOP
Shown at 25%; enlarge by 400% for actual size.

TOP (CUT 1)

BASE (CUT 1)

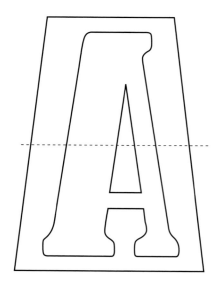

FRONT/BACK (CUT 2)

SIDE (CUT 2)

{AMPERSAND} BOOKENDS

Shown at 50%; enlarge
by 200% for actual size.

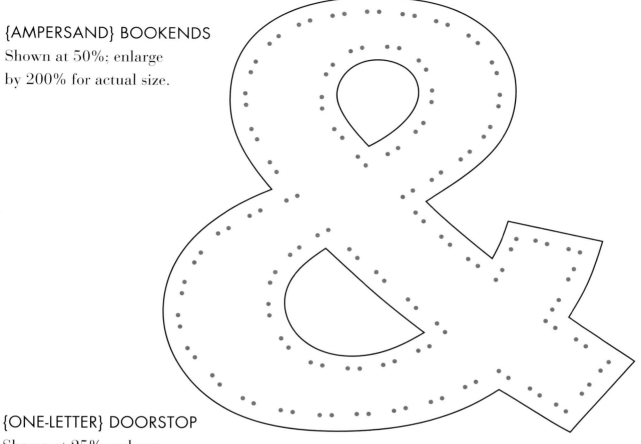

{ONE-LETTER} DOORSTOP

Shown at 25%; enlarge
by 400% for actual size.

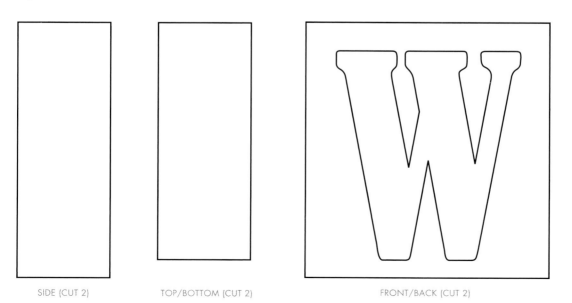

SIDE (CUT 2) TOP/BOTTOM (CUT 2) FRONT/BACK (CUT 2)

{SHINY-LETTER}
TOILETRY BAG

Shown at 70%;
enlarge by 143%
for actual size.

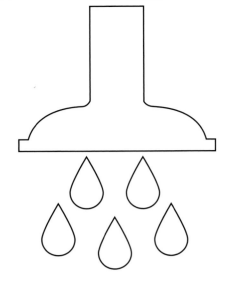

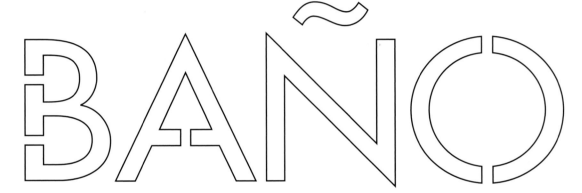

{LETTERED} CUSHIONS

Shown at 25%; enlarge by 400% for actual size.

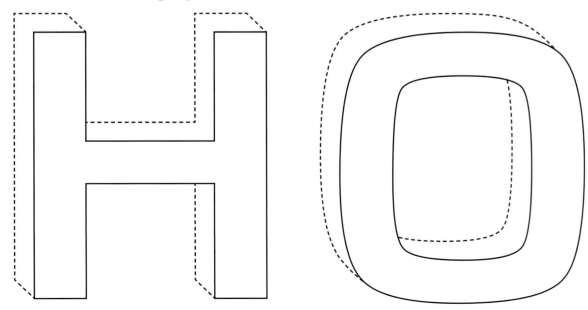

{LANGUAGE} POTHOLDERS

Shown at 70%; enlarge by 143% for actual size.

{CHEF'S} APRON

Shown at 70%;
enlarge by 143%
for actual size.

{CALLIGRAPHIC} TABLE RUNNER

Shown at 25%; enlarge by 400%
for actual size.

{CAFÉ} BLIND

Shown at 25%;
enlarge by 400%
for actual size.

{TABLET} CASE

Enlarge to match the size of your tablet.

{INITIALED} MESSENGER BAG

Shown at 25%; enlarge by 400% for actual size.

FLAP

FRONT OF BAG

BUBBLE SHAPE AND LETTER

SIDE OF BAG

BACK AND FRONT FLAP OF BAG

{BANNER} OF FLAGS

Shown at 25%; enlarge by 400% for actual size.

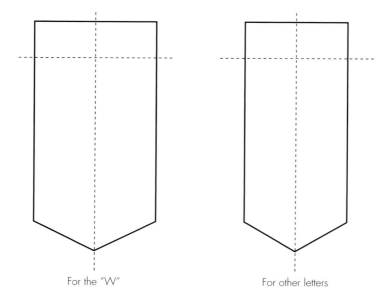

For the "W"   For other letters

Index